Earth-Friendly HOLIDAYS

Earth-Friendly HOLIDAYS

How to Make Fabulous Gifts and Decorations from Reusable Objects

George Pfiffner

John Wiley & Sons, Inc.
New York • Chichester • Brisbane • Toronto • Singapore

Copyright © 1995 by Tenth Avenue Editions, Inc.
Published by John Wiley & Sons, Inc.

The publisher and the author have made every reasonable effort to ensure that the experiments and activities in this book are safe when conducted as instructed but assume no responsibility for any damage caused or sustained while performing the experiments or activities in the book. Parents, guardians, and/or teachers should supervise young readers who undertake the experiments and activities in this book.

Library of Congress Cataloging-in-Publication Data

Pfiffner, George, 1923-
    Earth-friendly holidays : how to make fabulous gifts and
decorations from reusable objects / George Pfiffner.
             p.   cm.
    – (The Earth-friendly series)
     Includes bibliographical references.
     ISBN 0-471-12005-7 (paper : acid-free)
   1. Holiday decorations–Juvenile literature. 2. Handicraft–
Juvenile literature. 3. Recycling (Waste, etc.)–Juvenile literature.
4. Gifts–Juvenile literature. [1. Holiday decorations. 2. Handicraft.
3. Recycling (Waste)] I. Title. II. Series.
   TT900.H6P44   1995
   745.594'1–dc20   95-6584

Printed in the United States of America

10 9 8 7 6 5 4 3 2 1

Produced for John Wiley & Sons, Inc.
by Tenth Avenue Editions, Inc.
Creative Director: Clive Giboire
Assistant Editor: Matthew Moore
Editorial Assistants: Gene Aguilera, Judith Meyers
Artist: George Pfiffner
Assistant Artist: James Immes
Photographs: George Roos

Foreword

Every day when we open our mail at the Environmental Action Coalition, we find letters from young people all over the country. We have probably received a letter from your town, maybe even from your school.

Sometimes the letters ask questions, such as "How can we start a recycling program?" or "How does a landfill work?"

Sometimes they report on recycling projects kids have started, such as "We use both sides of our notebook paper" and "Our Boy Scout troop collected 392,000 cans."

We are always glad to get letters like these because we have been working on recycling since 1970, when only a few people were involved. Today people are coming up with more and more ideas about recycling.

Young people have made a big difference. You have come up with new ideas. Many of you have started recycling programs in your schools. You have taught your parents and grandparents how important recycling is, so the whole family can help keep the environment clean.

This is a very important moment in the history of the environmental movement. Young people all over the world are working together to try to save our planet from being buried under garbage.

As you can see from the globe on the cover of this book, you are part of an international movement. We all have a lot to learn from each other.

Have you heard the slogan **Reduce, Reuse, and Recycle**? These three simple words will give you the key to taking environmental action.

Reduce the amount of garbage you create. This means telling the person in the store that you don't need a bag to carry what you bought.

Reuse means finding a new life for something instead of throwing it away. That's what this book is all about.

Recycle means taking used materials and making them into materials that can be used again—like turning old newspaper into newspaper that can be printed on again.

Whether you are already an active recycler or are just getting started, this new series of books will give you many projects that you and your friends can make using things that would otherwise be thrown away.

If you enjoy the projects in this book, the next step is to show your friends how to make them.

You might also come up with some of your own ideas for projects. If you do, I'm sure the publisher would like to hear about them, so write them down. Who knows, maybe they'll be in the next book.

If you like the idea of recycling stuff, then you can look into what kind of recycling program your community has, or you can start a recycling program in your school. Ask your teacher for help.

But now it's time to get out your scissors and pencils and paste so you can get to work. Have a great time!

Steve Richardson
Executive Director
Environmental Action Coalition

Contents

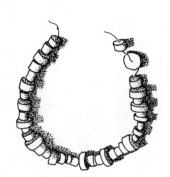

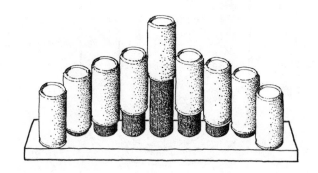

Being Earth-Friendly

Across the country and around the world, people are learning to reduce, reuse, and recycle. We have only one Earth, so we need to learn how to take care of it. We need to learn how to be "Earth-Friendly."

Some people think that recycling is just about washing out cans and tying up newspapers. But we think that recycling is really about rethinking—seeing the things around you in a new way.

When you start thinking about things in a new way, you can see that what used to be an old carrot is now a necklace, and what used to be a soda bottle is now a greenhouse. This book, and the other books in this series, are about using your imagination to make new things out of old "trash."

In this book, there are 29 holiday projects for you to make. Every project is made out of already used materials. As you learn how to make cool holiday projects, you will also be learning how to help the environ-ment. We've included information about recycling and tips on how you can help.

But the most important thing about this book is that it's fun! Every project in this book is fun to do. Even when you've made all the holiday projects in the book, the skills and ideas are yours forever. Who knows where your imagination will lead you.

Getting Started

Making your projects will be much easier if you follow all the instructions carefully. Here are some tips to get you started.

Before You Do Anything

Read all the instructions and look at the drawings **before** you start making a project. The more you know about how the project is made, the easier it will be to follow the steps.

Level of Difficulty

Each project is rated according to how easy it is to complete. Here's a key to the symbols used to rate each project:

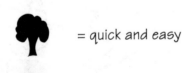 = quick and easy

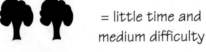 = little time and medium difficulty

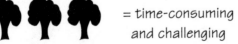 = time-consuming and challenging

You might want to start with some of the easier and faster projects until you get the hang of following the instructions.

Work Time

Set aside plenty of time to work on each project, and give it your full attention. Your holiday projects will turn out better if you don't hurry and if you aren't distracted.

Work Place

After choosing a project to make, decide on the best place to work. Some projects require more space than others. For example, the Globe (page 55) will need to dry undisturbed for several hours.

Materials

Before you start, get together everything you will need for the project. Put all the tools and materials on or near your work surface so that you can find them easily while you are working.

Some materials are easy to find at home. For some projects you will have to collect the materials you need from outside your home. Don't be discouraged if you don't have exactly the materials we suggest. In many of the projects you can substitute materials. Ask an adult helper to help you decide if a substitute will work.

Recycling Facts and Tips

Some projects have Recycling Facts and Tips at the end. These are ideas about how you can rethink and recycle every day.

Symbols You Will Need to Know

! Steps marked with an **!** need to be done with an **adult helper**. If you don't have an adult to help you, don't try this project.

✪ Even Better: This indicates ideas about how to make your holiday projects more interesting.

Have Fun!

Methods

The methods on the next few pages are shortcuts that are used in many of the projects. You may want to try them out before you start working on your first holiday project.

The Card Method will help you prepare old greeting cards to be used again.

The Envelope Method will help you make recycled envelopes for your recycled cards.

The Marbleizing Method will show you how to make paper look like marble.

The Pushpin Method is useful when you need to cut heavy material or when you need to cut "windows."

The Transfer Method will make it easy to transfer patterns from the book to paper, cardboard, or cloth.

The Glue Medium Method will show you how to make glue medium to strengthen fragile materials, like eggshells.

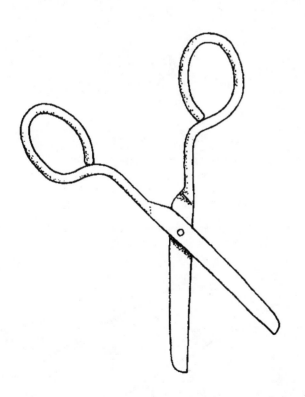 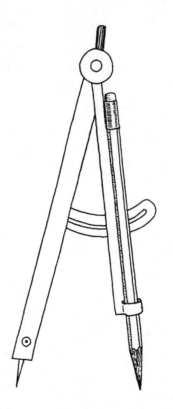 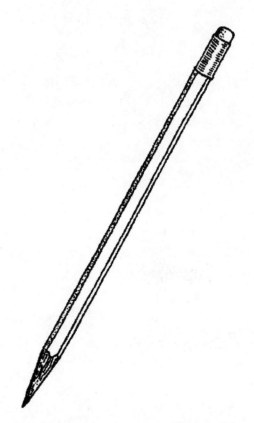

The Card Method

This method will help you prepare old greeting cards to be used again. You may want to cover several cards to use later.

You Need

❑ used or leftover greeting cards
❑ construction paper in several colors

Have on Hand

❑ stick glue

Tools

❑ a pencil
❑ a ruler
❑ scissors

Instructions

1. Place the card onto the corner of a piece of construction paper. Choose a color of construction paper that is close to the color of the card, or that contrasts nicely with the color of the card.

2. Use the pencil to draw around the outside of the card.

3. Use the scissors to cut along the lines you have just marked on the construction paper.

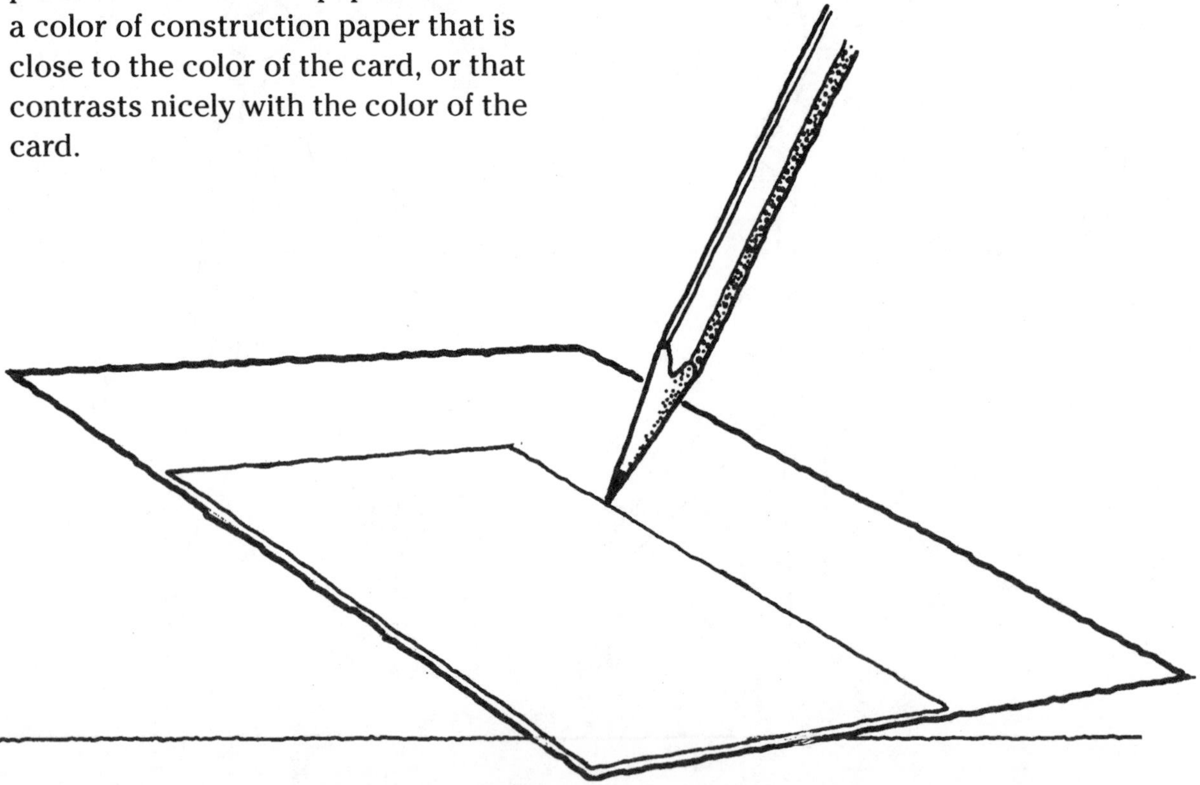

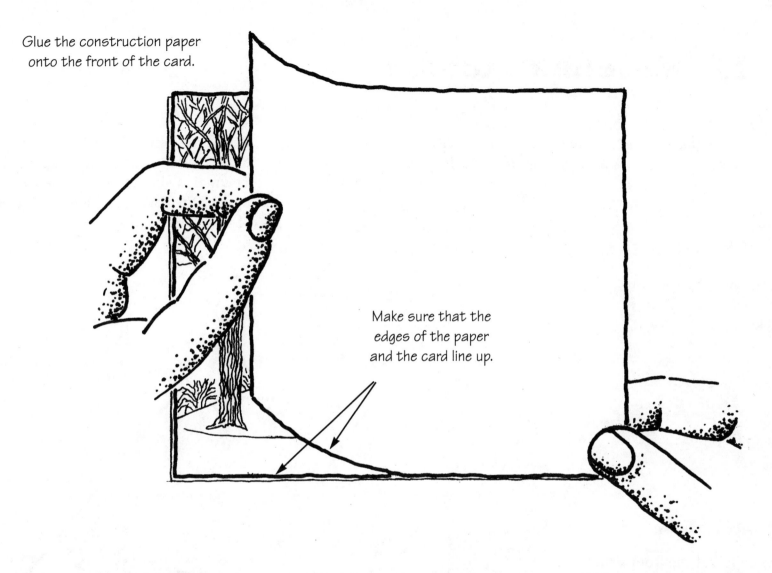

Glue the construction paper onto the front of the card.

Make sure that the edges of the paper and the card line up.

4. Coat the back of the cutout piece of construction paper and the front of the card with stick glue.

5. Glue the construction paper onto the front of the card. Make sure that the edges of the paper and the card line up. (If the edges do not line up exactly, use the scissors to trim the edges straight.)

6. Cut and glue a rectangle of paper to cover any writing inside the card. You could decorate this paper, and make up your own greeting.

The Envelope Method

This method will help you make recycled envelopes for your recycled cards.

You Need

❏ a large brown paper bag

Have on Hand

❏ tape

Tools

❏ a pencil
❏ a ruler

Instructions

1. Use scissors to cut the front panel off the bag.

2. Use the greeting card as a guide to make marks on the cutoff bag front. The marks should be 2½ times as high as the card and slightly wider, as shown.

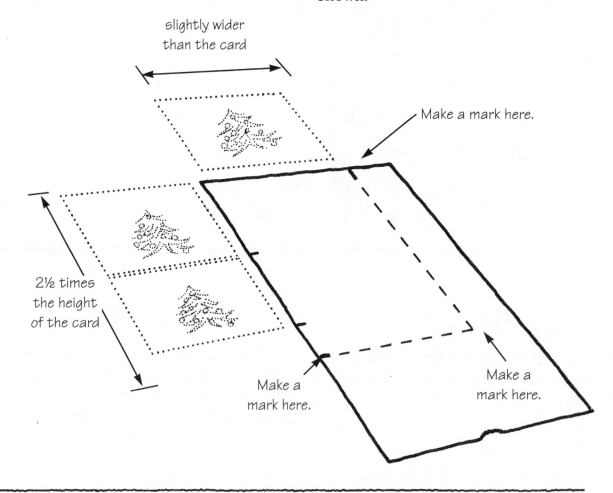

slightly wider than the card

2½ times the height of the card

Make a mark here.

Make a mark here.

Make a mark here.

3. Use the ruler and the pencil to draw lines onto the bag front connecting the marks you have just made. Make sure that the lines are as straight as possible.

4. Cut along the lines you have just marked.

5. To fold the envelope:

    a. Place the card onto the center of the brown paper.

b. Fold the bottom flap over the card and hold it in place.

c. Fold the top flap over the bottom flap.

6. To seal the card, tape the top flap to the bottom flap. Tape both sides closed.

7. Your recycled envelope is ready to be stamped, addressed, and mailed.

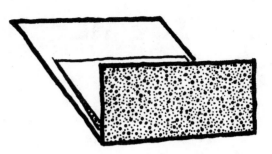

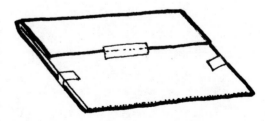

The Marbleizing Method

This method will show you how to make paper look like marble. "Marbleized" paper is used in several projects in this book, and it's also fun to make on its own. For the book projects, you will need about five sheets of marbleized paper, but you might want to make a few extras.

You Need

❏ 3 colors of any kind of **oil-based** paint: house paint or artist's paint

Note: Do not use acrylic or latex paint. Only oil paint will work for this project.

❏ paint thinner

❏ several pieces of construction paper

Have on Hand

❏ 3 small jars with lids, one for each color
❏ newspaper
❏ a shallow baking pan, 9 × 13 inches (22.5 × 32.5 cm);

it's OK to reuse a disposable pan if it has been carefully cleaned first
❏ water

Tools

❏ an old eyedropper (you will need to throw this away after completing this project)
❏ a fork
❏ a long needle
❏ a paint stirrer
❏ a pencil

! **Note:** Although this project is not difficult, paint and paint thinner are chemicals, and you should have an **adult helper** work with you for the whole project. **Do not** do this project if you do not have an **adult** to help.

Instructions

1. Cover your work area with several layers of newspaper.

2. Place the pan on your work surface. Fill the pan halfway with water.

3. Pour small amounts (just enough to cover the bottom of each jar) of the well-stirred paints into each small jar. Use a separate jar for each color.

4. Using the eyedropper, add paint thinner to each jar of paint, 3 or 4 drops at a time, until the paint is thinner, like heavy cream.

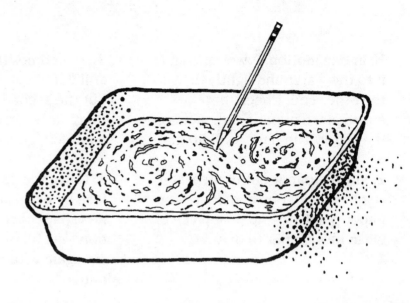

5. Dip the fork into one color of paint. Hold the fork over the pan of water and hit the fork with the pencil to spatter paint onto the water. Wipe off the fork, and repeat with the other two colors. Then you can make patterns in the paint:

a. Trail a pencil point (or a large needle) through the paint, always going in the same direction.

b. Use the pencil or needle to trace spirals, circles, or figure-eights through the paint floating on the water's surface.

6. When you like the way the paint floating on the water looks, it's time to dip your paper.

a. Pick up a piece of construction paper from opposite corners.

b. In one motion, lower one end into the water and lightly drop in the other end. Check that the entire piece of paper is touching the water. The paper will float.

c. Lift the paper out of the water right away by one end. Place the paper paint side up on a piece of clean newspaper to dry.

7. Sometimes there is enough paint still floating to cover a second sheet, but the second sheet will be paler. If there does not seem to be enough paint left, go on to the next step.

8. Clean the paint off the water's surface by dragging a piece of folded-up newspaper across the surface. If you don't get all the paint the first time, try again with a fresh piece of newspaper.

9. Make sure to clean up carefully. If you have paint left in the small jars, seal the lids tightly and you will be able to use the paint again later.

Lower one end into the water and lightly drop in the other end.

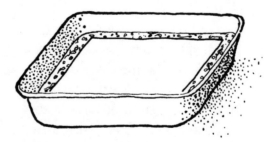

Lift the paper out of the water right away.

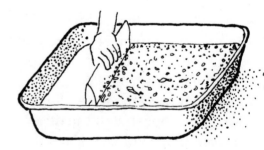

Clean the paint off the water's surface by dragging a piece of folded newspaper across the surface.

The Pushpin Method

*This method is useful when you need to cut
heavy material or when you need to cut "windows."*

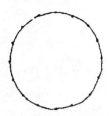

Punch holes at even intervals around the shape you want to cut.

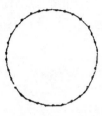

Then punch holes between those holes.

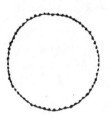

Then punch a third set of holes between those holes.

You Need

❑ a pencil
❑ a pushpin
❑ scissors

Instructions

1. Draw the line or shape to be cut.

2. Punch holes along the line or shape with the pushpin.

3. If the material you're cutting is **light** (such as light cardboard or thin plastic), you only need to make a few pushpin holes to start and guide the cut. Then use scissors to finish cutting.

4. If the material you're cutting is **heavy** and would be difficult to cut with scissors (such as heavy cardboard or thick plastic), you can make the entire cut with the pushpin alone.

a. Make pushpin holes at even intervals on the cut line, as shown.

b. Now make holes between those holes.

c. Then make a third series of holes between the holes you've already punched.

d. Once you've punched a lot of holes close together, you should be able to pull the pieces apart or push the shape out.

5. If you need to cut a square or rectangle, first mark each corner with a pushpin hole. Then make your other pushpin holes working from corner to corner.

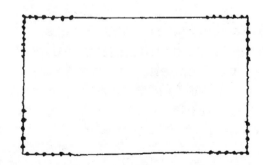

To cut right-angle corners, make pushpin holes along both edges.

The Transfer Method

For some of the projects in this book you will need to transfer patterns from the book to paper, cardboard, or cloth. This method will make that easy to do.

You Need

- ❏ a hard pencil
- ❏ a pencil sharpener
- ❏ a soft pencil
- ❏ tape
- ❏ tracing paper

Instructions

1. Working on a smooth, level surface, place the tracing paper over the design or pattern you want to transfer. Tape all four corners of the tracing paper to the pattern to keep the tracing paper from moving.

2. Trace the lines of the pattern onto the tracing paper using a soft pencil. Sharpen the pencil often so that the lines are clear and neat.

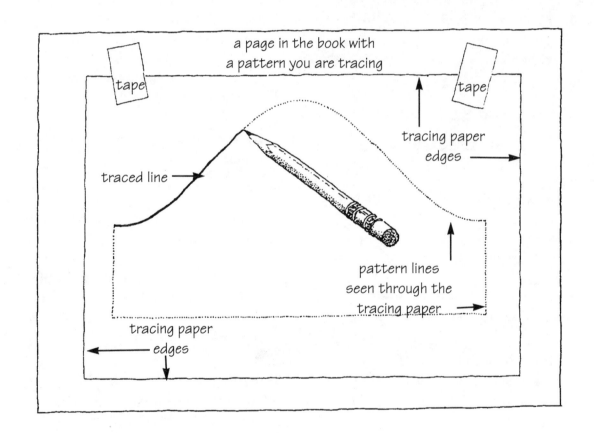

a page in the book with a pattern you are tracing

tape

tape

tracing paper edges

traced line

pattern lines seen through the tracing paper

tracing paper edges

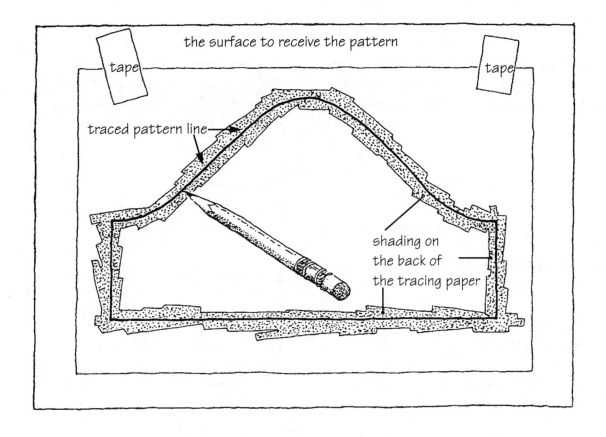

the surface to receive the pattern

tape

tape

traced pattern line

shading on
the back of
the tracing paper

5. Turn the tracing back over and tape it onto the surface you've selected for the pattern. Transfer the pattern to that surface by retracing over the lines, this time with the hard pencil. Be sure to go over each line carefully.

6. You can lift up a corner of the tracing paper to check that the pattern is being transferred clearly. If it isn't, add more shading with the soft pencil.

7. When the entire pattern has been transferred, you may want to darken the with a pencil.

3. When you have finished tracing the pattern, remove the tape and turn the tracing paper over.

4. Use a soft pencil to cover all the lines on the back side with pencil shading. Use the side of the pencil lead to make the shading.

The Glue Medium Method

Some of the materials you will use in projects in this book, like eggshells, are fragile. Coating them with glue medium will make them stronger and easier to work with. Acrylic matte medium will also work, if you have some at home.

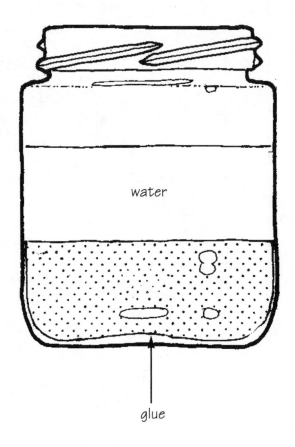

water

glue

You Need

- ❏ white glue
- ❏ water

Have on Hand

- ❏ a large jar with a lid, like a peanut-butter jar

Tools

- ❏ a fork

Instructions

1. Pour about 1 inch (2.5 cm) of glue into the jar.

2. Add about the same amount of water to the jar.

3. Stir the glue and water together thoroughly with the fork.

4. When you aren't using the glue medium, keep the jar sealed tightly with the lid. If the glue medium dries out or gets too sticky, add more water and stir it up again.

Valentine's Day

St. Valentine's Day is celebrated on February 14th. St. Valentine is the patron saint of lovers, and Valentine's Day honors love. Although this holiday probably originally comes from the Roman feast Lupercalis, which was celebrated on February 15th, it became connected to the feast day of two Roman Christian martyrs, both of whom were named Valentine.

Stencil Card

Express your affections with this colorful, recycled card.

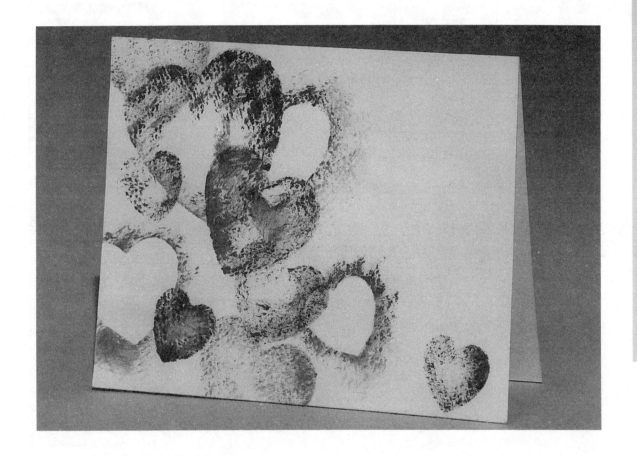

Instructions

1. Cut four 4-inch (10-cm) -square pieces from the manila file folder.

2. Draw a line down the center of each square piece.

3. Score the lines by firmly drawing the tip of the pushpin along them. Use a ruler to guide the pushpin.

4. Fold each square piece in half along the scored line.

5. Use the Transfer Method (see page 20) to transfer the four Heart Patterns below onto the square pieces.

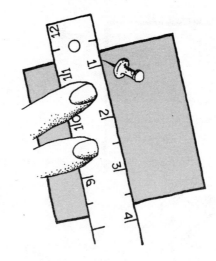

6. With the square pieces still folded, carefully cut out the hearts. Start your cuts at the folds. Save both the hearts and the squares.

7. Cover your entire work area with several layers of newspaper.

8. Pour a very small amount of one color of paint into one of the jar lids. Pour the same amount of the other paint into the other lid.

9. Use the cutout hearts and the "hollow" squares as stencils to paint heart shapes onto the recycled card in any pattern that you like.

Four
Heart
Patterns

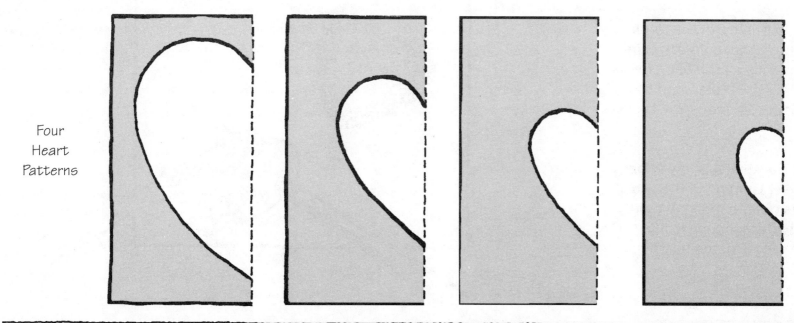

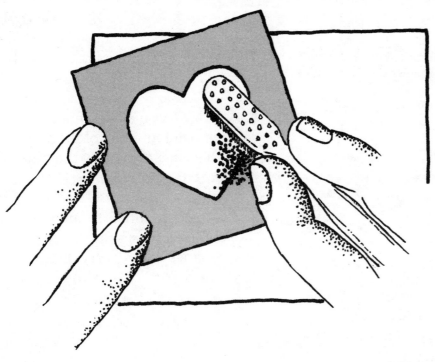

c. When you have dabbed all the way around the shape, carefully lift the stencil off the card. Let the paint dry before you paint another stencil.

d. If you want to change colors, make sure to wash the brush.

✪ **Even Better:** Stencil some small hearts onto the envelope you will use to send the card. (See the Envelope Method on page 14.)

a. Dip the bristles of the toothbrush into either color of paint. You want only a little paint on the brush. Dab the brush onto the newspaper to remove any excess paint.

b. Hold the stencil firmly in place with the eraser end of the pencil. With the other hand, dab **lightly** and **quickly** along the inside (or outside) edges of the heart shape.

Carrot Necklace

*Here's a great gift for any occasion.
It looks like coral, but it's really made from
the extra carrots in your refrigerator.*

You Need

- ❏ three or four carrots (these should be ready to be thrown out, but not rotten)
- ❏ a lemon

Have on Hand

- ❏ dental floss
- ❏ newspaper
- ❏ a small bowl

Tools

- ❏ a needle
- ❗ a paring knife
- ❗ a vegetable peeler

Instructions

1. Wash the carrots.

! 2. Have an **adult helper** peel the skin off the carrots with a vegetable peeler, cut the tops off the carrots with a paring knife, and cut the carrots into small pieces, about ¼ inch (.6 cm) wide.

! 3. Have an **adult helper** cut the lemon in half.

4. Squeeze the juice of the lemon into the small bowl.

5. Place the carrot pieces in the lemon juice. Stir the pieces so that all of them get covered with the juice. Leave the carrots in the juice for about 20 minutes. This will keep the carrots orange for a long time.

6. Hold your hand over the top of the bowl and pour out the lemon juice into a sink.

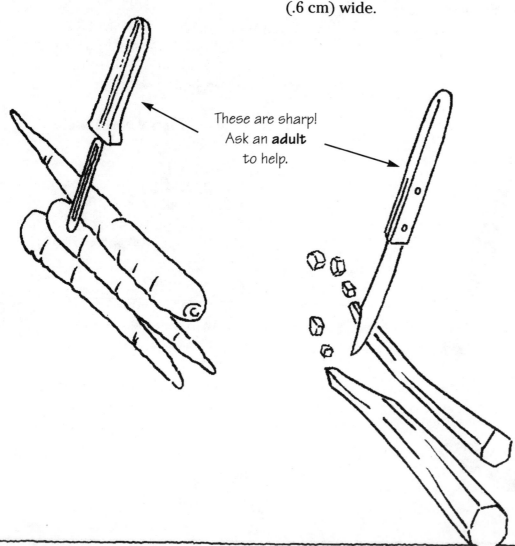

These are sharp! Ask an **adult** to help.

7. Cut a 30-inch (75-cm) piece of dental floss.

8. Thread the floss onto the needle.

9. String the carrot pieces onto the floss. You can make a pattern by mixing pieces of different sizes.

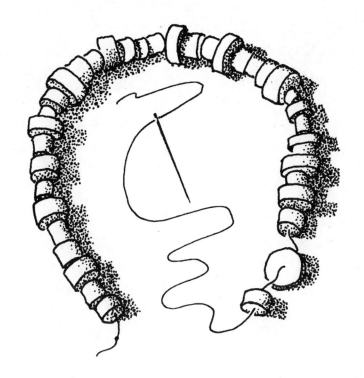

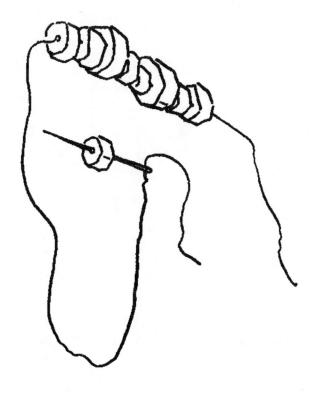

10. Place the string of carrots on newspaper and put it in a dry place. The carrots will take several days to dry completely. Check them every day to see if they are dry.

11. When the carrots are completely dry, push the pieces together. Tie the ends of the floss together and cut off any extra floss.

⊘ **Even Better:** You can thread old beads, or candies with holes in the middle, between the carrots.

Easter

Easter is a Christian holiday that celebrates the resurrection of Jesus Christ. Easter eggs and the Easter Bunny probably come from ancient European fertility traditions, which were celebrated in the spring.

Egg Card

The egg is a traditional symbol of Easter, reminding us of the rebirth that this holiday celebrates. These marbleized eggs are a beautiful way to celebrate this special day.

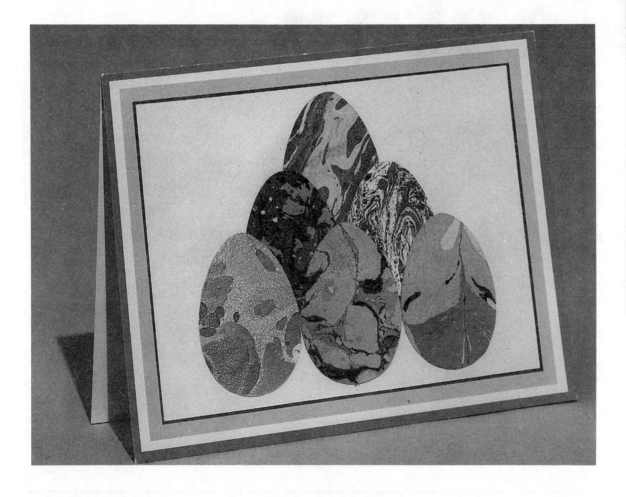

You Need

- ❏ marbleized construction paper (see the Marbleizing Method on page 16)
- ❏ a recycled card (see the Card Method on page 12)

Have on Hand

- ❏ scrap cardboard
- ❏ stick glue

Tools

- ❏ a pushpin
- ❏ a ruler
- ❏ scissors

Instructions

1. Cut out a piece of cardboard 3 × 2¼ inches (7.5 × 5.5 cm).

Egg Shape Pattern

2. Draw a lengthwise line down the center of the cardboard.

3. Score the line by drawing the tip of the pushpin along it firmly. Use a ruler to guide the pushpin.

4. Fold the cardboard in half on the scored line.

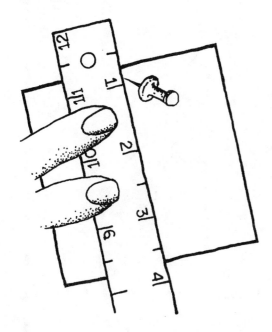

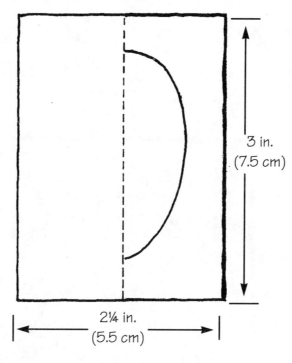

3 in.
(7.5 cm)

2¼ in.
(5.5 cm)

5. Use the Transfer Method (see page 20) to transfer the Egg Shape Pattern above onto the cardboard, with the dotted line on the fold.

6. With the cardboard still folded, carefully cut out the egg shape pattern. Start your cut at the fold, and be sure to cut through both halves of the paper at the same time.

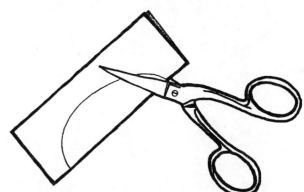

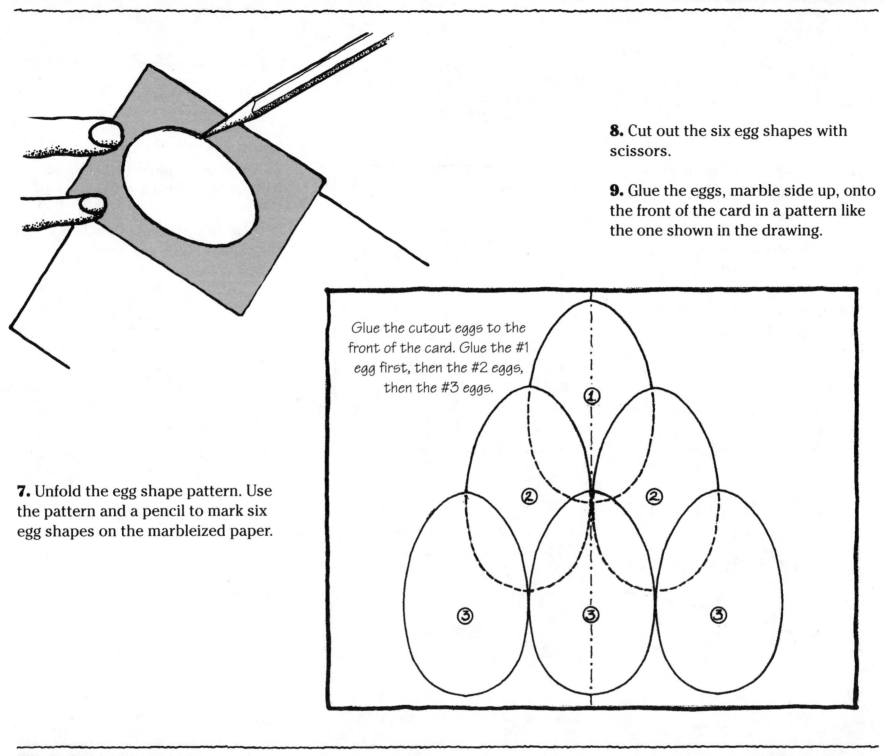

8. Cut out the six egg shapes with scissors.

9. Glue the eggs, marble side up, onto the front of the card in a pattern like the one shown in the drawing.

7. Unfold the egg shape pattern. Use the pattern and a pencil to mark six egg shapes on the marbleized paper.

Glue the cutout eggs to the front of the card. Glue the #1 egg first, then the #2 eggs, then the #3 eggs.

① ② ② ③ ③ ③

Woven Basket

Colorful baskets have been a part of the Easter tradition for a long time. This pretty container is useful, and it's made from a reused berry basket and some old plastic bags.

You Need

❑ two plastic grocery bags in different colors

❑ a plastic berry basket, 1 pint (.5 liter) size

Have on Hand

❑ double-sided tape

Tools

❑ scissors

Instructions

1. Cut four strips of plastic 18 inches (45 cm) long and about 3 inches (7.5 cm) wide from one bag. These are the A strips.

2. Cut one strip the same size from the second bag. This is the B strip.

3. Cut one strip of plastic that is 4 inches (10 cm) wide and 8 inches (20 cm) long. This will be the handle.

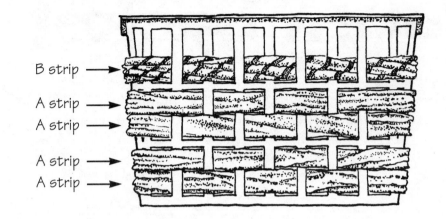

B strip →
A strip →
A strip →
A strip →
A strip →

4. Weave one of the A strips in and out through the holes near the bottom of the basket until it meets itself. Always go around the **outside** of the corners, even if you need to skip a weave.

a. Tape the two ends of the strip together inside the basket, using double-sided tape.

b. Cut off any excess plastic from the strip.

5. Weave three more A strips into the basket above the first strip. Alternate the weaves, so that where the first strip goes inside, the second strip goes outside.

6. Weave the B strip into the basket.

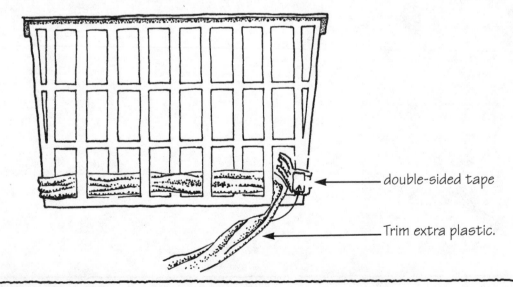

← double-sided tape

← Trim extra plastic.

7. Thread one end of the last strip of plastic through the center of one side of the basket. Tie the end of the strip in a knot. Pull the knot tight and fan out the extra plastic.

✪ **Even Better:** You can glue a piece of cardboard to the bottom of the basket if you want to keep small things in it.

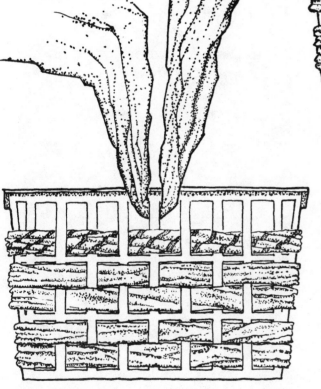

8. Repeat step **7** with the other end of the last plastic strip on the opposite side of the basket.

9. Your basket is complete. You can fill it with candies, eggs, or whatever you want.

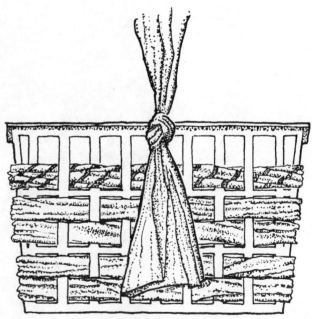

Pull the knot tighter and spread out the end.

Eggshell Centerpiece

Here's a way to give your Easter eggs a new look. A few eggshells, a flowerpot, and some bamboo skewers can be transformed into a beautiful decoration for your holiday table.

You Need

- ❑ one dozen or more eggshell halves (Use the largest shells you can collect.)
- ❑ bamboo shish-kebab skewers
- ❑ a small flowerpot or tin can
- ❑ sand or pebbles

Have on Hand

- ❑ glue medium (see the Glue Medium Method on page 22)
- ❑ a glue brush
- ❑ marking pens in several colors
- ❑ a rubber eraser
- ❑ scrap cardboard (such as from a cereal box)

Tools

- ❑ a long needle
- ❑ small scissors

Instructions

1. Carefully wash the eggshells inside and out. Remove the membrane from inside the shells as best you can.

2. To strengthen the shells, brush the inside of each shell with three coats of glue medium. Be sure to let each coat dry for ten minutes before applying the next coat. Let the last coat dry for ten minutes.

3. Decorate each shell with marking pens both inside and out.

4. Place the rubber eraser on your work surface and rest a shell on it. Use the needle to gently nick a small hole on the inside bottom of the shell.

5. Insert the tip of a bamboo skewer into the hole in the shell. Gently spin the skewer between your fingers to make the hole slightly larger.

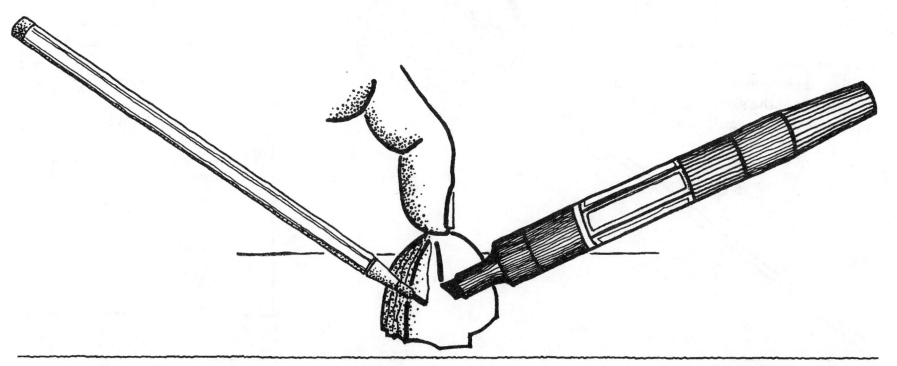

6. Repeat steps **4** and **5** with each shell.

7. Cut a ½-inch (1.3-cm) -square piece of cardboard.

8. Place the square on the eraser and use the pin to make a hole in the center of the square.

9. Place the square on the point of a bamboo skewer and push it about 1 inch (2.5 cm) onto the skewer.

10. Trim the cardboard square into a circle with the scissors.

11. Put a dab of glue on top of the cardboard circle and slip the eggshell onto the tip of the skewer so that it rests on top of the cardboard.

12. Place sand in the flowerpot or tin can. Stick the skewers into the sand to dry.

13. Repeat steps **7–12** for the other shells, and your centerpiece is done.

Recycling Facts & Tips

Did you know that:

- The U.S. throws away 500,000 tons (450,000 t) of trash every day.
- This much trash would fill nearly 92 million lunchboxes!

How you can help:

- Wrap your sandwich in aluminum foil, which can be recycled, not in plastic wrap, which can't.
- Bring drinks to school in a thermos, rather than in disposable containers like juice packs or cans.

Passover

The Hebrew name for this holiday is pesah, *which means "passing over." Pesah refers to God's instruction to the Israelites in captivity in Egypt to mark their doors with lamb's blood so that the angels who had come to kill the first-born sons of the Egyptians would "pass over" their houses. Passover is celebrated on the 14th day of Nisan in the Jewish calendar. This is roughly the same time as the vernal equinox, the day in the Spring when the sun is directly over the equator, about March 21st.*

Star Card

Celebrate the Passover spirit of hospitality and generosity by sending someone this beautiful, recycled card.

Circle Pattern

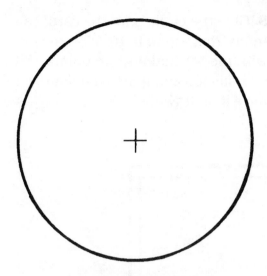

5. Use the Transfer Method to transfer the Star Pattern to one half of the paper back of the foil. Make sure to line up the fold with the edge of the pattern, as shown.

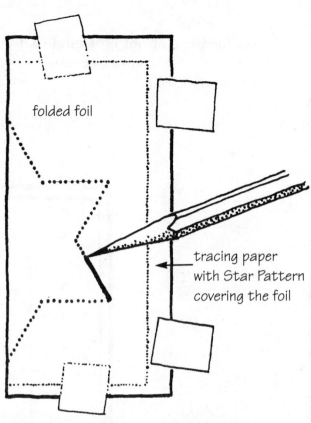

folded foil

tracing paper with Star Pattern covering the foil

Make sure to line up the fold in the foil with the edge of the Star Pattern.

Instructions

1. Use the Transfer Method (see page 20) to transfer the Circle Pattern onto the blue paper.

2. Cut out the paper circle.

3. Lightly crumple the foil, then smooth it back out. This gives the foil an interesting texture.

4. Fold the foil in half so that the paper back of the foil shows.

Star Pattern

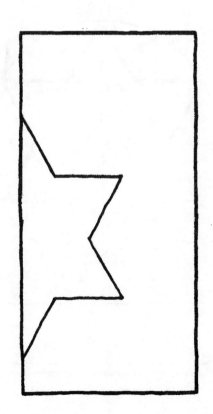

6. Use the scissors to cut out the foil star. Make sure to cut through both halves of the foil at the same time. Unfold the foil star.

7. Glue the star onto the circle with stick glue. Make sure to center the star in the circle.

8. Measure and mark the middle of the fold of the card. Make another mark in the middle of the opposite edge. Use the ruler and pencil to draw a faint line connecting the two marks you have just made.

9. Glue the circle onto the card, centered from top to bottom on the card, with the top and bottom points of the star aligned along the guideline you have just drawn.

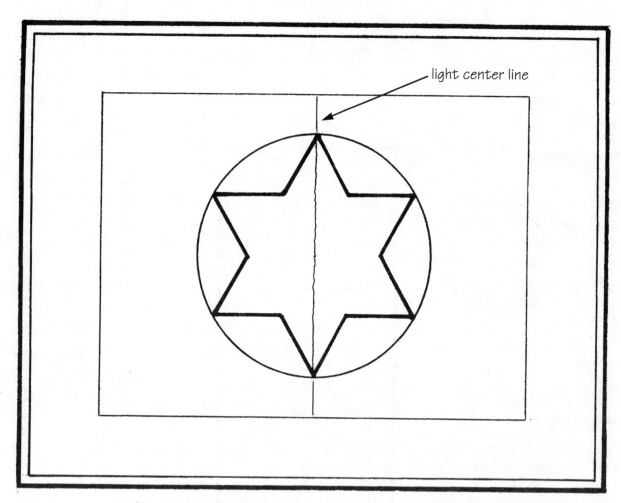

light center line

Glue the circle onto the card, centered from top to bottom.

Matzo Cover

Matzo, *an unleavened bread (bread made without yeast or other ingredients to make it rise), symbolizes the bread that the ancient Israelites ate on the Exodus out of Egypt to the Promised Land. The Israelites had to eat unleavened bread because they fled Egypt so quickly that the bread they had been baking didn't have time to rise. Matzo is eaten at the Passover seder, a ritual meal that symbolically reenacts the captivity and exodus of the Israelites.*

You Need

- ❑ three pieces of 8 × 9-inch (20 × 22.5 -cm) marbleized paper and one piece of 8 × 8-inch (20 × 20-cm) marbleized paper (see the Marbleizing Method on page 16)
- ❑ a piece of scrap white drawing paper

Have on Hand

- ❑ a black marking pen

Tools

- ❑ a pencil
- ❑ scissors
- ❑ stick glue

Instructions

1. Fold over 1 inch (2.5 cm) of one 8-inch (20-cm) end of each of the three 8 × 9-inch (20 × 22.5-cm) pieces of paper. Fold two of these ends blank-side to blank-side and one marble-side to marble-side.

2. Label the piece that you folded marble-side to marble-side B. Label the other two pieces A and C. Label the unfolded 8 × 8-inch (20 × 20-cm) piece of paper D.

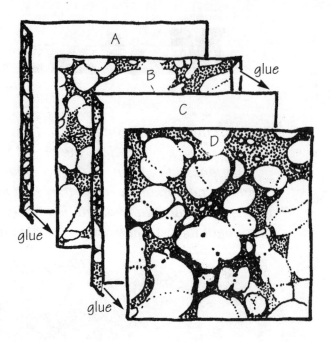

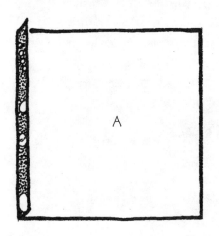

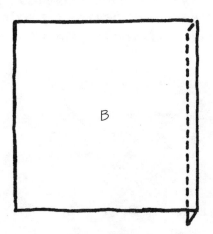

Each sheet has
its blank side up.

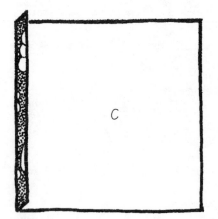

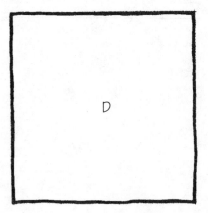

3. Glue the marble side of the folded end of piece A to the blank side of the unfolded end of piece B.

4. Glue the blank side of the folded end of piece B to the marble side of the unfolded end of piece C.

5. Glue the marble side of the folded end of piece C to the blank side of one end of piece D.

8. Glue the blank side of the scrap paper to the marble side of either piece A or piece D.

9. When you are ready for the Passover seder, insert the matzo into the cover as shown.

6. Tear the edges of the scrap paper to make it look antique.

7. Use the marking pen to draw the Hebrew word Matzo onto the piece of scrap paper. See the drawing above as a guide.

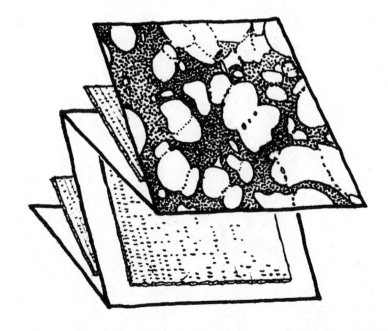

Earth Day

Earth Day takes places every April 22nd. It is a day set aside to remind ourselves of the need to protect the planet. Earth Day is a relatively new holiday—it was first celebrated in 1970.

Veggie Card

Vegetable prints will really put the person who gets this card in the Earth Day spirit.

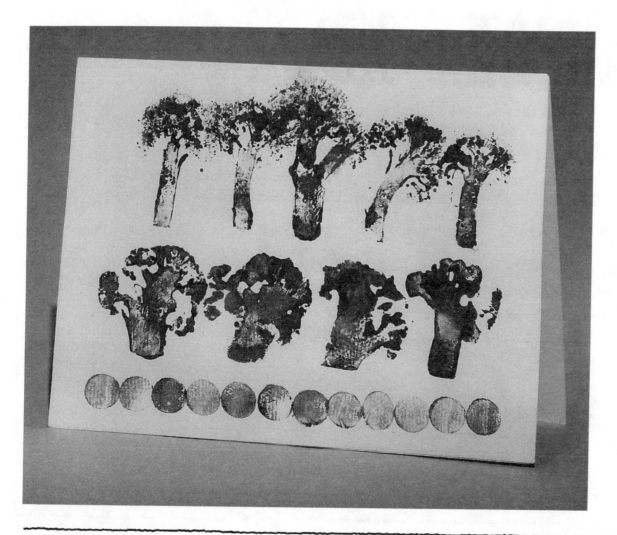

You Need

- ❏ one stem of broccoli
- ❏ one stem of cauliflower
- ❏ one small carrot
- ❏ green and yellow poster paints
- ❏ a recycled card (see the Card Method on page 12)
  Note: Use the biggest card you can find.

Have on Hand

- ❏ an old jar lid
- ❏ newspaper

Tools

- ❏ a butter knife
- ❗ a kitchen knife
- ❏ a pencil
- ❏ a ruler

Instructions

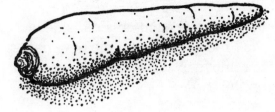

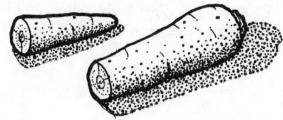

! 1. Ask an **adult helper** to use the kitchen knife to cut four cauliflower branches and five broccoli stems that look like small trees. Ask the **adult helper** to cut each stem in half, as shown.

whole pieces   sliced pieces

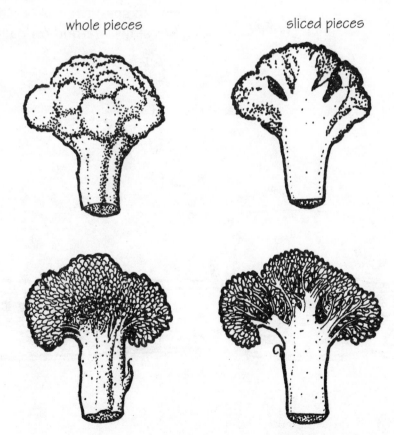

! 2. Ask an **adult helper** to slice off a small piece of carrot. The top piece that would otherwise be thrown away is fine.

3. Cover your entire work surface with several layers of newspaper.

4. Use the butter knife to put a little green poster paint in the jar lid. Put an even smaller amount of yellow in with the green. Mix the paints together to make a light green color.

5. Press the flat side of one of the broccoli branches into the paint.

6. Stamp the paint-covered side of the broccoli down on the newspaper to remove excess paint. Then stamp on the card.

7. Repeat with the rest of the broccoli, then with the cauliflower, and finally with the carrot slice. Follow the pattern shown in the photo at the beginning of this project, or create your own design.

✪ **Even Better:** Add some veggie stamps to the envelope you will use to send the card (see the Envelope Method on page 14).

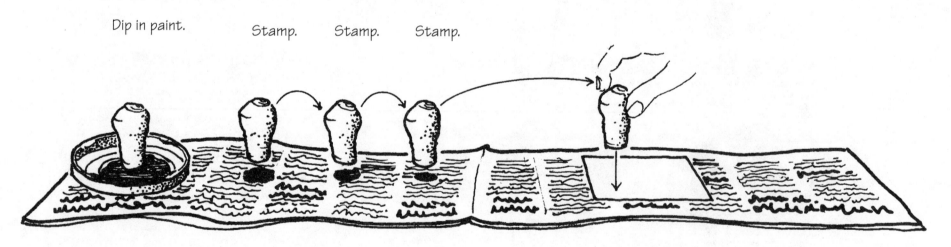

Stamp the card.

Dip in paint.

Stamp. Stamp. Stamp.

Bottle Greenhouse

You can sprout an avocado plant from a pit, using a recycled soda bottle to make a miniature greenhouse.

You Need

- ❏ one avocado pit, washed
- ❏ three toothpicks
- ❏ an empty jar, with a mouth large enough for the avocado pit to fit in
- ❏ a clear plastic 2-liter soda bottle

Have on Hand

- ❏ water

Tools

- ❏ a pushpin
- ❏ scissors

Instructions

1. Remove and recycle the colored plastic bottom (if there is one) from the bottle. You should be able to pull it off, or you can cut it off with scissors.

2. Use the Pushpin Method (page 19) and scissors to cut the top off the soda bottle. Cut along the top of the label.

3. Remove the label.

4. Break the three toothpicks in half. Stick three toothpick halves into the sides of the avocado pit, as shown.

5. Rest the toothpicks on top of the jar, with the point of the pit inside the jar.

6. Fill the jar with water until the pit is at least half covered.

7. Place the jar on a windowsill where it will get some sunlight. Cover the jar with the cut-apart soda bottle.

8. Make sure that the pit is always half-covered with water.

9. When the pit develops a lot of roots and a few leaves, transplant it into soil in a pot.

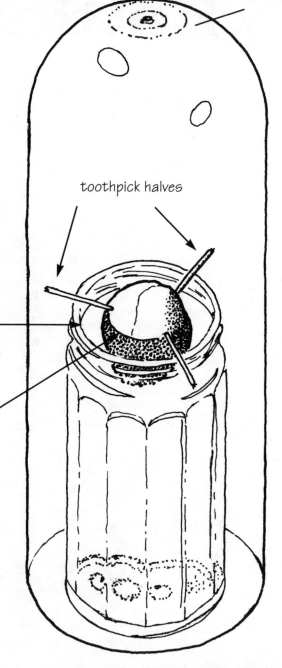

bottom of soda bottle

toothpick halves

avocado pit

water halfway up the pit

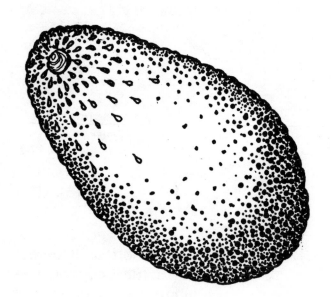

Globe

Sometimes it's hard to remember how big the Earth is and how much work there is to be done to keep it from being polluted or buried in garbage. This recycled globe will be a friendly reminder to "think globally."

You Need

- ❏ a rubber ball that has lost its bounce, about 5 inches (12.5 cm) in diameter
- ❏ black-and-white newspaper
- ❏ colored newspaper, such as the comics section
- ❏ light blue tissue paper
- ❏ bright green construction paper
- ❏ string

Have on Hand

- ❏ a friend to help
- ❏ glue medium (see the Glue Medium Method on page 22)
- ❏ a large jar with a lid
- ❏ masking tape
- ❏ waxed dental floss

Tools

- ❏ a glue brush
- ❏ scissors

Instructions

Note: This project is messy, and it will need to dry undisturbed for a couple of hours. Check with an adult that the work area you have chosen is OK for this project. Cover your entire work area with several layers of newspaper. You may also want to wear old clothes that can get dirty.

1. Tape dental floss around the seam on the ball, leaving 6 inches (15 cm) of extra floss at both ends.

2. Tear several sheets of newspaper (both black-and-white and colored) into narrow strips. Tear the strips into small rectangles. Keep the black-and-white and colored pieces separate.

3. Brush one side of a piece of black-and-white newspaper with glue medium.

4. Brush glue medium onto a small area of the ball.

5. Stick the piece of newspaper onto the ball, glue side down. Brush more glue medium over the laid-down strip.

6. Repeat steps **3–5** to cover the entire ball. As you cover the ball, make sure that the ends of the dental floss stick out through the newspaper.

7. Leave the ball to dry for one hour.

8. Repeat steps **3–7** with a layer of colored newspaper.

9. Repeat steps **3–7** again with another layer of black-and-white newspaper. Let this layer dry for a half hour.

10. Tear the blue tissue paper into narrow strips.

11. Apply glue medium to a small portion of the sphere and stick torn tissue paper onto the glue. Smooth the tissue paper down and brush more glue medium on top of it. Cover the entire sphere.

12. While a friend holds the ball, pull both ends of the dental floss gently but firmly, so that the floss slowly tears through the newspaper.

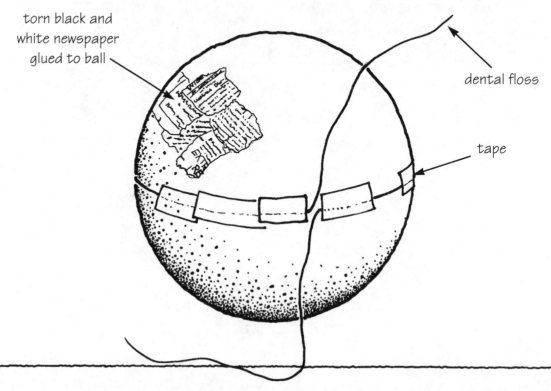

torn black and white newspaper glued to ball

dental floss

tape

13. Pull back each half of the paper ball, but do not divide the globe into two separate pieces: Just make an opening large enough to remove the ball.

14. Have a friend hold the two paper half-globes together. Cover the seam with one layer of glued-on tissue. Do not worry if the seam is still visible.

15. Transfer the Continent Pattern (page 58) onto the green construction paper. Be sure to transfer the line representing the Equator too.

16. Cut out the continents from the construction paper.

17. Glue the continents onto the globe with the glue medium. Line up the Equator line with the seam you covered in step **14**.

18. Make a pushpin hole in the top of the globe. Enlarge the hole with the point of a pencil. Don't make the hole too big: It needs to be small enough that a knot in the string will not easily slip through it.

19. Make a knot in one end of the string. Push the knot through the hole you just made. You may need to use the pushpin to push the knot through.

20. Put a bit of glue down into the hole along with the string so that the knot doesn't pull through. Let the glue dry for 10 minutes, and you can hang the globe by the string.

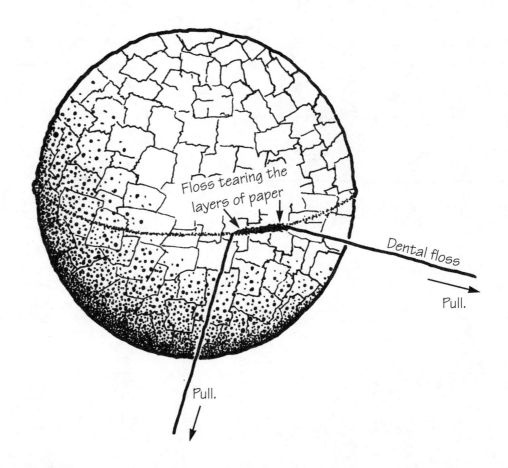

Floss tearing the layers of paper

Dental floss

Pull.

Pull.

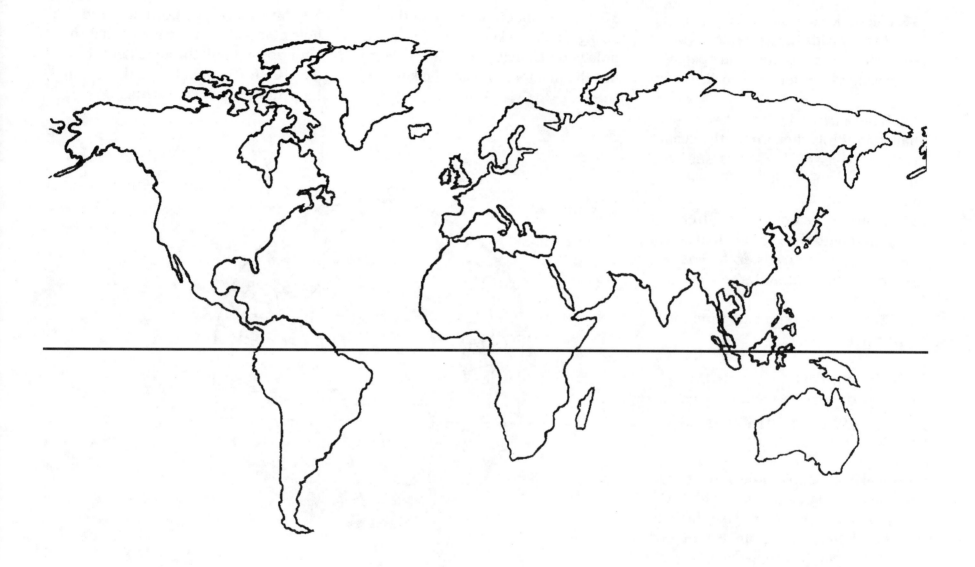

Continent Pattern

Mother's Day

Mother's Day is celebrated on the second Sunday in May.
It is a special day set aside to honor mothers.

Fabric Card

This beautiful card is great for Mother's Day.

Instructions

Note: For this project, you should cut a piece of paper to cover the front of the card, but don't glue it down before you start the project.

1. Fold the piece of paper, which you have cut to cover the front of the card, in half. Open the paper, then fold it in half the other way, making quarter sections.

2. Cut the scraps of fabric so that they are slightly larger than the quarter sections of paper.

3. Glue a piece of tissue paper to the back of each piece of fabric. Make sure to rub stick glue on both the paper and the fabric.

4. Trim the rectangles of fabric so that they are exactly the same size as the quarter sections of paper.

5. Cut four pieces of fabric diagonally in one direction.

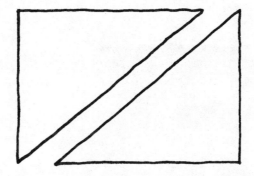

6. Cut four pieces of fabric diagonally in the other direction.

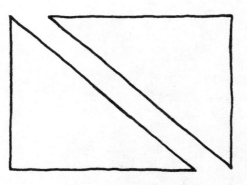

7. Unfold and smooth out the piece of paper you folded in step **1**.

8. Glue the triangles to the paper, two triangles in each quarter section of paper.

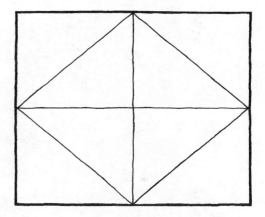

9. Glue the back of the paper to the front of the used card.

✪ Even Better: You can make a second card with the leftover fabric triangles.

Balloon Vase

This beautiful vase, filled with dried flowers or leaves, makes a perfect Mother's Day gift.

You Need

- ❑ one balloon
- ❑ string, 30 inches (75 cm)
- ❑ one paper-towel tube
- ❑ newspaper
- ❑ colored newspaper, such as the comics section
- ❑ construction paper in six or seven colors (scraps of paper are fine)
- ❑ gold foil, such as from candy bars
- ❑ one piece of light, flexible cardboard, ¾ × 12 inches (1.9 × 30 cm)
- ❑ two cups of sand or pebbles

Have on Hand

- ❑ a bowl of warm water
- ❑ glue medium (see the Glue Medium Method on page 22)
- ❑ a heavy book
- ❑ a jar with a lid, such as a peanut-butter jar
- ❑ a large soup can
- ❑ a large jar, such as a mayonnaise jar

Tools

- ❏ a glue brush
- ❏ masking tape
- ❏ a pushpin
- ❏ scissors

Instructions

1. Blow up the balloon and tie a knot in the end.

2. Tie the center of the string above the balloon knot.

3. Make two pairs of scissor cuts on opposite sides of one end of the paper-towel tube.

4. Drop the two ends of the string down through the uncut end of the tube. Pull the balloon down against the opposite end of the tube. Slip the strings into the slits at the bottom of the tube to hold the balloon tightly against the top of the tube.

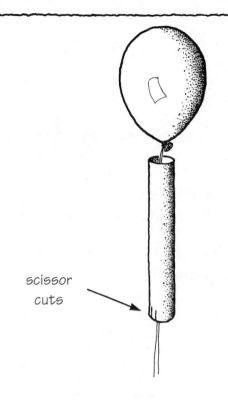

scissor
cuts

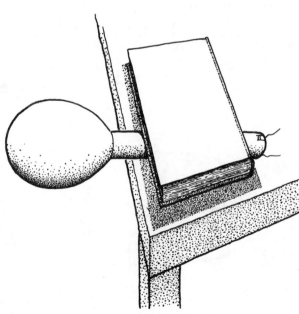

5. Lay the tube on the edge of a table, so that the balloon is hanging over the edge. Place the book on the tube so that it holds the tube and balloon in place. Place several layers of newspaper on the floor below the balloon.

6. Tear several sheets of newspaper (both black-and-white and colored) into narrow strips. Tear the strips into small rectangles. Keep the black-and-white and colored pieces separate.

7. Brush one side of a piece of black-and-white newspaper with glue medium.

8. Brush glue onto a small area of the balloon.

9. Stick the piece of newspaper onto the balloon, glue side down. Brush more glue over the laid-down strip.

10. Repeat steps **7–9** to cover the entire balloon.

11. Leave the balloon to dry for one hour.

12. Repeat steps **7–9** with a layer of colored newspaper.

13. Repeat steps **7–9** again with another layer of black-and-white newspaper. Let this layer dry for a half hour.

14. Tear the construction paper into strips 1½ inches (3.7 cm) wide. Place the strips in the bowl of warm water for 10 minutes to soften them.

15. Repeat steps **7–9** with the strips of construction paper. Blot the strips on some newspaper to remove excess water. Let this layer dry for a half hour.

16. Repeat steps **7–9** with bits and pieces of gold foil.

17. Place the strip of light cardboard in the bowl of water for about 20 minutes to soften it. Blot the cardboard on some newspaper to remove as much excess water as you can.

18. Wrap the damp cardboard around the large can and tape it in place with masking tape. Leave this in place overnight to dry. Once the strip is dry, carefully remove it from the can.

19. Glue the ends of the strip together to make a circle.

20. Decorate the cardboard circle with glued-on pieces of construction paper.

21. Stand the paper-towel tube in the large, empty jar. Glue the cardboard circle to the top of the balloon with white glue. Let the glue dry for about 30 minutes.

22. Remove the paper-towel tube from the large jar. Untie the strings from the end of the tube, and discard the tube.

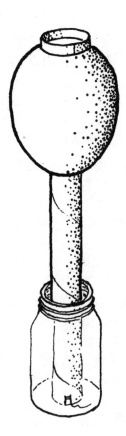

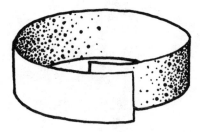

23. Use the pushpin to puncture the balloon near the knot you tied in step **1**. Pull the balloon out from inside the paper shell.

24. Use the scissors to cut a neat, circular opening around the knot where the balloon was. Use the hole in the paper where the tube was as a guide.

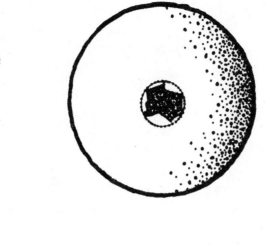

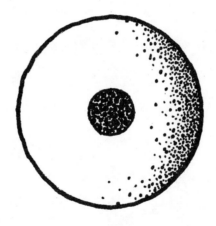

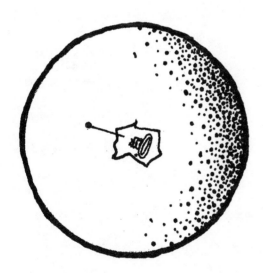

25. Place sand or pebbles in the vase to keep it from tipping over.

26. Stand your vase up on its base. It's ready to be filled with dried flowers.

Did you know that:

- Nearly 35% of the trees cut every year become paper.
- If we recycled half the paper we use each year, we would cut 20 million fewer acres of forest.

How you can help:

- Try to buy less packaging. For example, do you need a bag for everything you buy? Use your backpack or tote bag instead.
- Some foods—like rice, beans, pasta, cereal, and even candy—are available "in bulk." That means you can buy them without a lot of packaging.

Father's Day

Father's Day is celebrated on the third Sunday in June.
It is a special day to honor fathers.

Lettered Card

Your D-A-D will love this card made out of magazine pictures and your cutout message. And he'll love knowing that it's made out of recycled materials.

You Need

- ❏ a recycled card (see the Card Method on page 12) **Note:** A larger card is better for this project.
- ❏ a picture of something your dad likes cut from a magazine. (The picture should be a little larger than your card and should not have any writing or type on it.)

Have on Hand

- ❏ stick glue

Tools

- ❏ a pencil
- ❏ a ruler
- ❏ scissors

Instructions

1. Lay the card down in one corner of the cutout picture.

2. Use the pencil to trace around the outside of the card.

3. Cut along the lines you have just marked.

4. To fold up the cutout picture:

  a. Fold it in half lengthwise (side to side). Crease it and mark the ends of the creases with the pencil.

  b. Unfold the picture. Use the ruler and pencil to draw a thin line connecting the marks you have just made.

  c. Fold each half of the picture (on either side of the line you have just drawn) in half lengthwise (sides to the middle). Crease the picture and mark the ends of the creases with a pencil.

  d. Unfold the picture. Use the ruler and pencil to draw a thin line connecting the marks you have made.

  e. Repeat steps **a** and **b**, this time folding from end to end.

  f. Repeat steps **c** and **d**, this time folding from end to end.

  g. Finally, repeat step **f**, folding the four tall sections in half and marking their crease lines.

5. Cut the picture into pieces along the lines you have just drawn. As you cut them apart, lay the pieces onto your work surface in order.

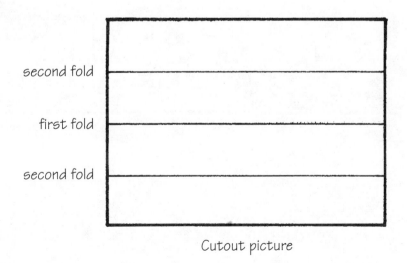

Cutout picture

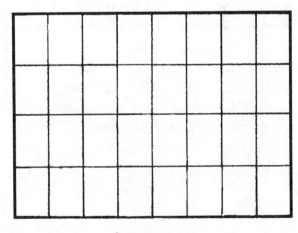

Cutout picture

6. Select the pieces of the picture that are going to be letters, using the drawing as a guide. Cut the letters TO A GREAT DAD out of these pieces. Use the photograph at the beginning of this project as a guide for cutting the letters.

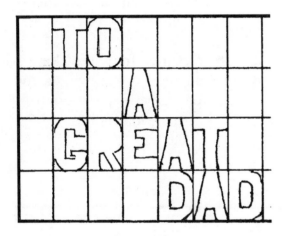

7. Glue the pieces of the picture to the card. Start with the pieces around the edges, then work toward the center. The card will look better if you leave irregular spaces between the pieces.

Bookmark

Personalize this bookmark by covering it with pictures of whatever your dad enjoys most: flowers, sports, sunsets, sailboats, fishing, movies, or pictures of his favorite city or country.

You Need

- ❑ a piece of clear adhesive plastic, 3 × 8 inches (7.5 × 20 cm) (You can buy this at a hardware store.)
- ❑ small pictures of whatever your dad likes cut from magazines
- ❑ a piece of colored adhesive plastic, 3 × 8 inches (7.5 × 20 cm) (also available at a hardware store)

Tools

- ❑ scissors

Instructions

1. Lay the piece of clear adhesive plastic on your work surface, but don't remove the protective paper from the sticky side.

2. Arrange the pictures on the clear plastic into a pattern you like. Each picture should slightly overlap the ones next to it.

3. Remove the protective paper from the sticky side of the colored plastic and place the plastic on your work surface, sticky side up.

4. Keeping the pattern you laid out on the clear plastic, move the small pictures one by one onto the colored plastic, so that they are face up. Make sure to stick the backs of the pictures down firmly onto the plastic.

Note: If you make a mistake, move the pictures right away.

5. Use the scissors to trim one edge of the bookmark straight, cutting off the pieces of the pictures that extend past the edge of the plastic.

6. Remove the protective paper from the clear plastic and place it sticky-side down over the pictures, lining it up with the trimmed edge.

7. Press the clear plastic into place. Trim the other three edges straight. Rub your fingers over the bookmark to remove any air bubbles.

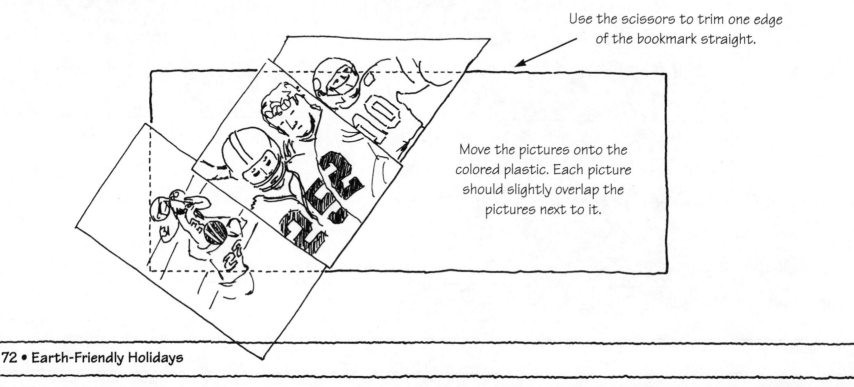

Use the scissors to trim one edge of the bookmark straight.

Move the pictures onto the colored plastic. Each picture should slightly overlap the pictures next to it.

Halloween

Halloween is celebrated on the night of October 31st, the day before the traditional Christian feast called Allhallows, *or* All Saint's Day. *The word* Halloween *is short for* All Hallow's Eve. *Historians think that the modern Halloween holiday comes from an ancient Druid festival that celebrated the end of the year (on the Druidic calendar) and warded off evil spirits. The idea of ghosts, goblins, and other spirits wandering around is still part of Halloween today, and the jack-o'-lantern is our way of scaring them away.*

Pumpkin Card

This jack-o'-lantern card made from a potato print is great for inviting your friends to a Halloween party.

You Need

❑ one recycled card (see the Card Method on page 12)

Have on Hand

❑ newspaper
❑ an old jar lid
❑ one raw potato
❑ orange poster paint
❑ scrap cardboard

Tools

❑ a dull pencil
❑ an old emery board or nail file
! a sharp knife
❑ a sharp pencil

Instructions

! 1. Ask an **adult helper** to cut a 1-inch (2.5-cm) -wide slice of potato with a sharp knife. It is very important that the cuts be smooth and straight.

2. Use the Transfer Method (see page 20) to transfer the Pumpkin Pattern below onto the scrap cardboard.

3. Cut out the cardboard pumpkin.

4. Hold the cardboard against one side of the slice of potato. Draw around the outline of the pattern with the sharp pencil. You will have to push down hard on the pencil to make a mark you will be able to see later.

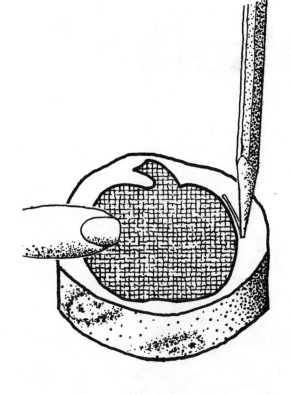

5. Use the pencil to cut and break away the potato outside the outline you have just drawn. Cut jack-o'-lantern eyes, a nose, and a mouth in the pumpkin. You don't need a pattern—just cut them freehand.

6. Pour a little paint into the jar lid. You don't need a lot.

7. Press the cut end of the potato into the paint. Stamp the paint-covered potato onto the newspaper to remove any excess paint.

8. Stamp the potato onto the front of the recycled card several times in any pattern you like. You will need to repeat step **7** before each stamp.

9. Use the emery board to file the tip of the dull pencil into a small, flat circle.

10. Dip the point of the pencil into the paint. Dab the paint into the eye holes to make eyeballs and along the mouth to make teeth.

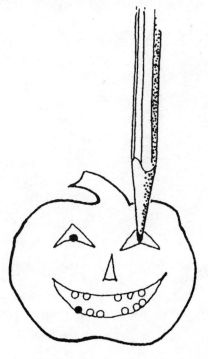

Pumpkin Pattern

Bird Mask

This Halloween, go dressed as a bird with a mask made from reused materials. You can celebrate Earth Day and Halloween at the same time with this beautiful mask!

You Need

- ❑ two white paper plates, 9 inches (22.5 cm) across
- ❑ one paper-towel tube
- ❑ scrap cardboard

Have on Hand

- ❑ a brown marking pen
- ❑ orange and brown poster paint
- ❑ a rubber band
- ❑ a small paintbrush
- ❑ string, 14 inches (35 cm)
- ❑ white glue

Tools

- ❑ a hole punch
- ❑ a pencil
- ❑ a pushpin
- ❑ a ruler
- ❑ scissors

Instructions

1. Cover the back of the rim of one plate—about 2 inches (5 cm) in from the edge—with brown poster paint. Let the paint dry completely before going on to the next step.

2. Glue the front of the uncolored plate to the back of the plate you have just colored, covering the rim you have just painted. Glue together only the center, flat section of the plates, not the raised rims.

3. Use the Transfer Method (see page 20) to transfer the Face Pattern (page 80) onto the flat section of the uncolored plate.

4. Use the Pushpin Method (see page 19) and scissors to cut out the eyes and the beak hole.

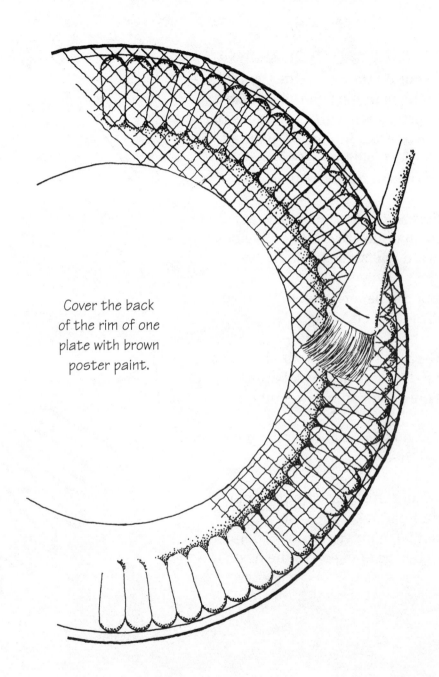

Cover the back of the rim of one plate with brown poster paint.

5. Decorate the rim of the top plate with the marking pen to look like feathers, as shown. Cut the rims of the two plates into small, pointed feathers. It will be easiest if you cut both rims at the same time.

6. Spread the feathers apart and bend them in opposite directions—some forward and some back.

7. Cut the paper-towel tube down to 9 inches (22.5 cm) long.

8. Use the Transfer Method (see page 20) to transfer the Beak Pattern (page 81) onto the paper-towel tube.

9. Cut out the beak from the paper-towel tube.

10. Paint the beak with the orange poster paint. Let the paint dry for about 20 minutes (or until completely dry) before going on to the next step.

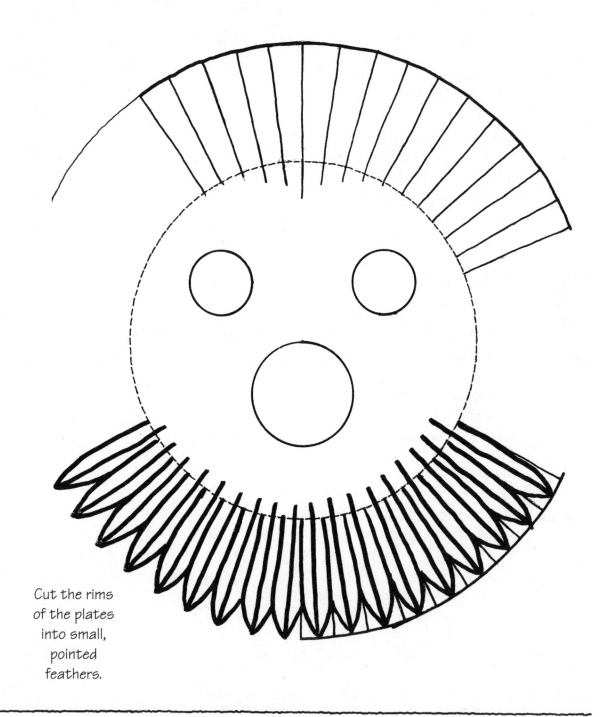

Cut the rims of the plates into small, pointed feathers.

11. Apply white glue to about ½ inch (1.3 cm) of the wide end of the beak.

12. Slide the beak into the beak hole from the back of the mask (the "front" of the plates), narrow-end first.

13. Apply a little more glue around the beak on both the front and back of the mask.

14. Set the mask down on its back on your work surface for 15 minutes while the glue dries.

15. Cut the string in half.

16. Tie one end of each piece of string to the rubber band.

17. Cut two small rectangles, about ½ × 1 inch (1.3 × 2.5 cm), from the scrap cardboard. Fold these in half lengthwise to make brackets.

18. Punch a hole in the center of one half of each bracket.

19. Glue the halves of the brackets without holes onto the back of the mask on either side of the beak, closer to the rims than to the beak hole. Let the glue dry for about 10 minutes before you go on to the next step.

20. Tie the loose ends of the strings through the holes in the brackets.

21. Put the mask on your head.

Apply more glue around the end of the beak.

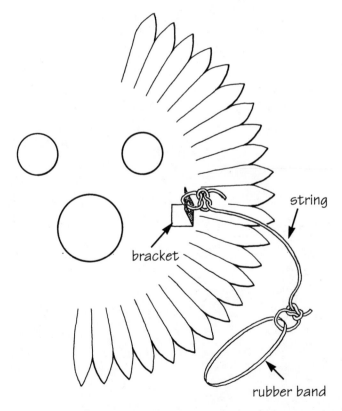

string

bracket

rubber band

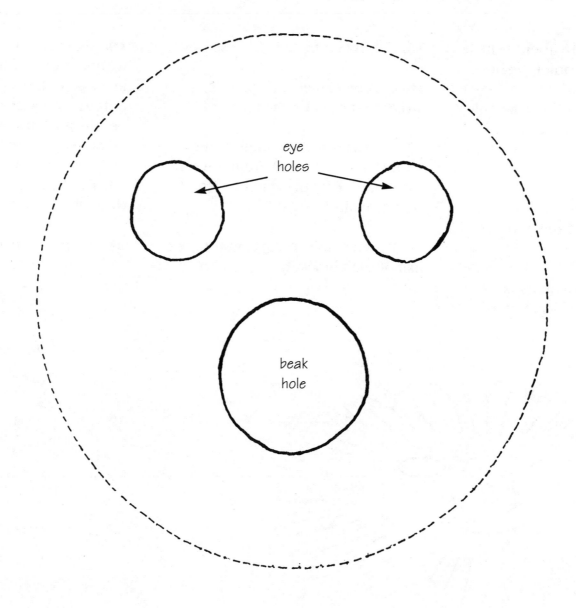

eye
holes

beak
hole

Face Pattern

Beak Pattern

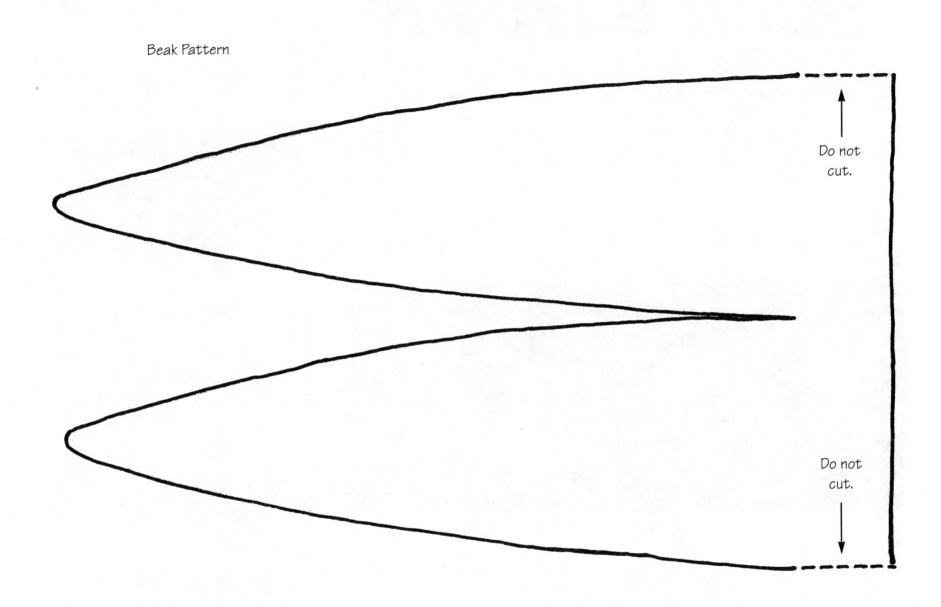

Do not cut.

Do not cut.

Skull Garland

These scary skulls are the ideal decoration for your haunted house. One bleach or detergent bottle will make a string of four skulls. For more, just find more bottles.

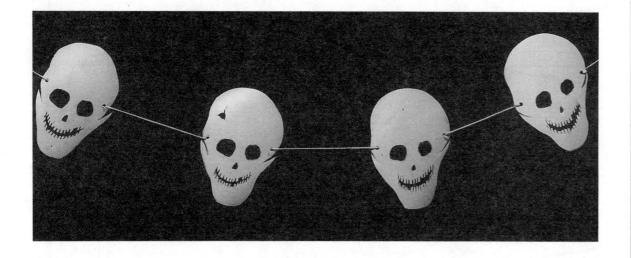

You Need

❗ one empty 1-gallon (3.8-liter) white plastic bottle, like the kind bleach or laundry detergent come in (Ask an **adult helper** to clean out the bottle before you use it.)
❑ string

Have on Hand

❑ a marking pen
❑ scrap cardboard

Tools

❑ embroidery scissors
❑ an eraser
❑ a hole punch
❑ a pushpin
❑ scissors

Instructions

1. Use the Pushpin Method (see page 19) and scissors to cut off the top and bottom of the bottle. Cut along the ridges near the top and bottom, as shown. Recycle the cutoff plastic.

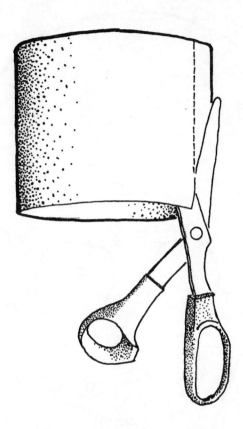

4. Transfer the cardboard skull pattern to the plastic four times with the marking pen.

5. Use the Pushpin Method and scissors to cut out the plastic skulls.

6. Cut teeth in each skull with embroidery scissors.

7. Use the hole punch to make a hole on either side of the skull, near where the ears would be.

8. Thread the skulls onto the string. Loop the string around each hole so the skulls don't slide around on the string.

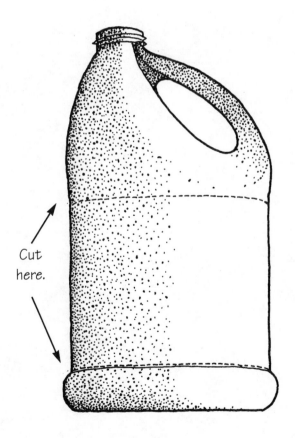

Cut here.

2. Make one cut along the length of the bottle, as shown.

3. Use the Transfer Method (see page 20) to transfer the Skull Pattern (page 84) onto the scrap cardboard. Make sure to cut out all the areas marked on the pattern.

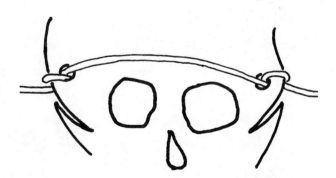

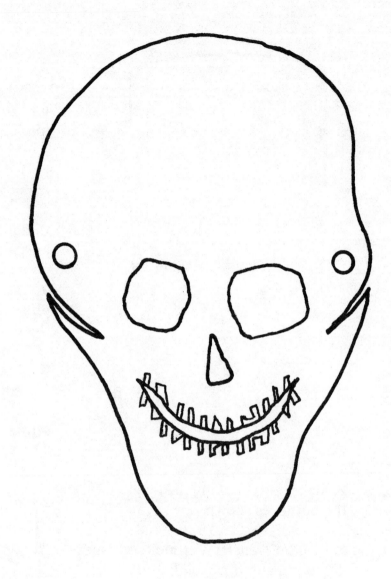

Skull Pattern

Thanksgiving

*Thanksgiving is celebrated on the second Monday in October in Canada and the fourth
Thursday in November in the United States. Although the Thanksgiving tradition
was begun by the Pilgrims as a celebration of their successful harvest,
it is probably based in older harvest festivals. Thanksgiving
became widely celebrated in the late nineteenth century
in both the United States and Canada.*

Turkey Card

This is a great card to give or send around Thanksgiving. Gobble, gobble!

You Need

- ❏ a recycled card (see the Card Method on page 12)
- ❏ tracing paper
- ❏ marking pens, colored pencils, or crayons

Have on Hand

- ❏ an 8½ × 11-inch (21.3 × 27.5-cm) piece of scrap paper
- ❏ masking tape
- ❏ stick glue

Tools

- ❏ a black marking pen
- ❏ an eraser
- ❏ a pencil
- ❏ scissors

Instructions

1. Use the scissors to cut a piece of tracing paper slightly larger than the Turkey Pattern.

2. Tape the tracing paper flat over the Turkey Pattern.

3. Trace the pattern and the border with a pencil. (Don't use a pen.)

4. Place the tracing paper on the scrap paper. Go over the tracing lines with a black marking pen.

5. Color the turkey any way you like. (We used shades of brown and gray.)

6. Cover the front of the recycled card with stick glue. Place the tracing paper onto the front of the card, using the border around the image to make sure that the image is square on the card.

7. Use the scissors to trim away any excess tissue from around the edges of the card. Erase any pencil lines that still show.

Turkey Pattern

Leaf Garland

This autumn garland makes a beautiful decoration for Thanksgiving or any fall occasion. It's easy to make, and it brings the fall colors inside.

You Need

❏ heavy, twisted cord
Note: Sisal cord is the best kind of cord to use. You can buy it at a hardware store. Do not use braided cord.
❏ a lot of fall leaves (See the note on page 89.)

Have on Hand

❏ a bucket
❏ masking tape
❏ ¾ cup (177 ml) of glycerin (You can buy this at a drug-store.)
❏ water

Tools

❏ a pencil
❏ scissors

Instructions

Note: In most of the United States and Canada the leaves will have already fallen weeks before Thanksgiving. To make this garland, collect leaves and twigs when they have just fallen and are still flexible.

To keep the leaves and twigs from drying out, mix ½ gal. (1.9 liter) of water and ¾ cup (177 ml) of glycerin in a bucket. Stand the leaves stem down in the bucket in a shaded place outdoors for about five days. The colors will change a little, but the leaves will stay flexible for a long time.

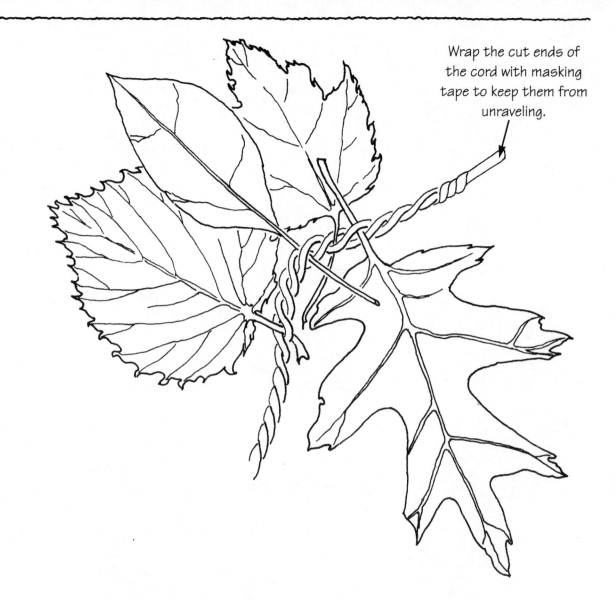

Wrap the cut ends of the cord with masking tape to keep them from unraveling.

1. Cut a length of cord as long as you want your garland to be. Wrap the cut ends with masking tape to keep them from unraveling.

2. Starting at one end, untwist part of the cord. Insert a leaf stem or twig through the strands of the cord every 1 inch (2.5 cm) or so along the length of the cord.

3. When you have placed leaves along the entire length of the garland, fill in any thin places.

4. Hang or arrange the garland where you wish.

Hanukkah

Hanukkah, *which means "dedication" in Hebrew, begins on the 25th day of* Kislev, *the third month in the Jewish calendar (roughly the same time of year as December). Hanukkah celebrates the rededication of the Temple of Jerusalem, after Judas Maccabee took it back from Syrian king Antiochus IV Epiphanes. The rededication required pure olive oil to be burned for eight days, but there was only one day's supply available. Miraculously, the oil burned for eight days. This miracle is represented by the eight candles of the Hanukkiyah.*

Hanukkiyah Card

Menorah *is the Hebrew word for candelabra, which is a branched candlestick or lamp with several lights. A menorah used for Hanukkah is called a* hanukkiyah. *The central candle, which is used to light the others, is called the* shammos. *The other eight candles represent the eight days of the miracle of the Festival of Lights.*

You Need

- ❏ gold foil with a paper back, such as from a candy bar
- ❏ a recycled card (see the Card Method on page 12)

Have on Hand

- ❏ stick glue

Tools

- ❏ a hole punch
- ❏ a pencil
- ❏ a ruler
- ❏ scissors

Instructions

1. Cut a piece of foil that is 5 × 2½ inches (12.5 × 6.3 cm). Lightly crumple the foil, then smooth it back out. This gives the foil an interesting texture.

2. Fold the length of the piece of foil in half, so that the paper back of the foil is on the outside.

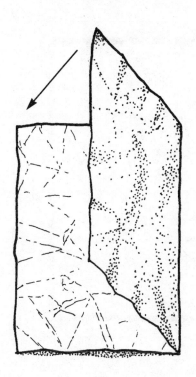

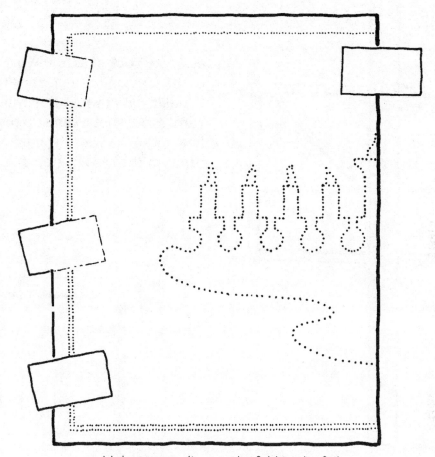

Make sure to line up the fold in the foil with the edge of the Hanukkiyah Pattern.

3. Use the Pattern Transfer Method (see page 20) to transfer the Hanukkiyah Pattern (page 94) to one half of the paper back of the foil. Make sure to line up the fold with the edge of the pattern.

4. Use the scissors to cut out the foil hanukkiyah. Use the hole punch to make the round cuts between the candles. Make sure to cut through both halves of the foil at the same time. Unfold the foil hanukkiyah.

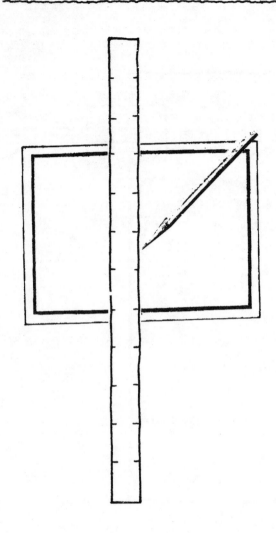

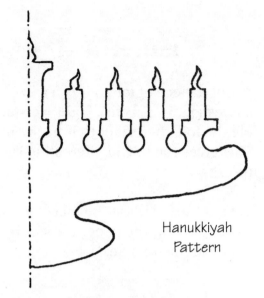

6. Apply stick glue to the paper back of the foil hanukkiyah. Stick the hanukkiyah down to the front of the card. Make sure to line up the fold line in the foil with the guideline you drew on the card in step **5**.

Hanukkiyah Pattern

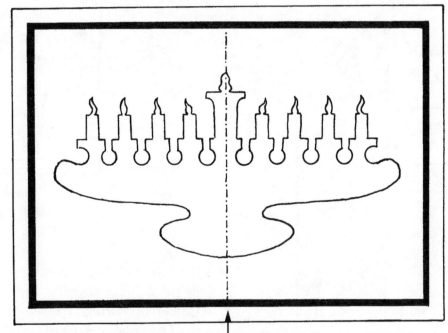

5. Measure and mark the middle of the fold of the card. Make another mark in the middle of the opposite edge. Use the ruler and pencil to draw a faint line connecting the two marks you have just made.

Make sure to line up the fold in the foil with the guideline on the card.

Dreidel

Dreidel is an old game of chance. The Hebrew characters
nun gimmel heh shin *stand for the Hebrew phrase*
"Nes gadol hayah sham," *which means*
"A great miracle happened there."

You Need

❑ a piece of heavy cardboard,
  3 × 3 inches (7.5 × 7.5 cm)
❑ a sharp pencil

Have on Hand

❑ a black marking pen

Tools

❑ a pushpin
❑ a ruler

Instructions

1. With the ruler and pencil, draw diagonal lines from corner to corner on one side of the cardboard.

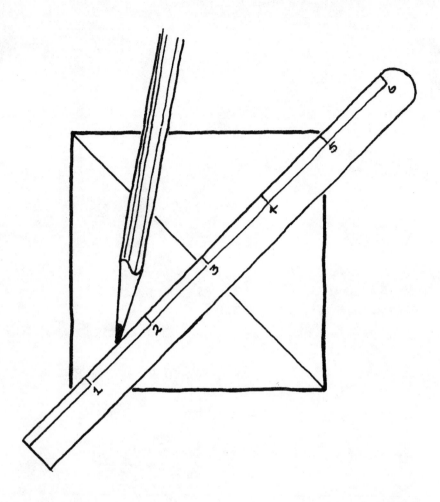

5. Your Dreidel is ready to play. Here's how:

    a. Each player starts with the same number of coins or counters (you could use bottle tops).

    b. Each player puts one counter from his or her pile into a pile in the middle (the "pot"). Each time a player takes a turn, he or she adds another counter to the pot.

2. Use the Transfer Method (see page 20) to transfer the Dreidel Pattern (page 97) onto the piece of cardboard. Line up the diagonal lines you have just drawn with the lines in the pattern.

3. Use the marking pen to darken the diagonal lines and the Hebrew characters on the dreidel.

4. Use the pushpin to make a small hole where the diagonal lines cross. Use the sharpened pencil to enlarge the hole so that the pencil fits snugly in the hole, then push the pencil eraser down through the hole in the cardboard. About half the pencil should be above the cardboard, and about half below.

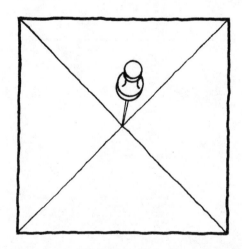

c. Each player spins the dreidel in turn. If you get:

(nun): Do nothing; the next player spins the dreidel.

(gimmel): Take the whole pot. Everyone puts one counter in to make a new pot and the next player spins.

(heh): Take half the pot (or half plus one if the pot is an odd number).

(shin): Put one counter into the pot.

d. When the pot is empty, or if there is only one counter in the pot, every player puts one counter into the pot before the next player spins.

e. The game is over when one player wins all the counters.

Hanukkiyah

Make your own Hanukkiyah deocoration for a perfect Hanukkah gift.

You Need

- ❏ nine small, clean, and empty juice cans, 5.5-oz. (163-ml) size (They must all be the same size and type.)
- ❏ clean, used aluminum foil (enough to cover all of the cans)
- ❏ one paper-towel tube
- ❏ bright blue paper
- ❏ a piece of stiff cardboard or wood, roughly 20 inches (50 cm) long and 3½ inches (8.8 cm) wide

Have on Hand

- ❏ an old jar lid
- ❏ stick glue
- ❏ white glue

Tools

- ❏ a pencil
- ❏ a ruler

Instructions

1. Cover the sides of the cans with foil, using stick glue.

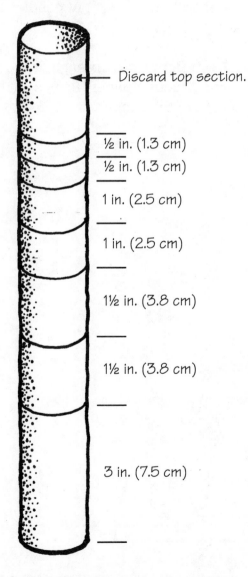

Discard top section.

½ in. (1.3 cm)

½ in. (1.3 cm)

1 in. (2.5 cm)

1 in. (2.5 cm)

1½ in. (3.8 cm)

1½ in. (3.8 cm)

3 in. (7.5 cm)

2. Measure and make marks along the paper-towel tube, as shown in the diagram:

a. Make one mark 3 inches (7.5 cm) from the bottom of the tube.

b. Make a second mark 1½ inches (3.8 cm) from the mark you have just made.

c. Make a third mark 1½ inches (3.8 cm) from the mark you have just made.

d. Make a fourth mark 1 inch (2.5 cm) from the mark you have just made.

e. Make a fifth mark 1 inch (2.5 cm) from the mark you have just made.

f. Make a sixth mark ½ inch (1.3 cm) from the mark you have just made.

g. Make a seventh mark ½ inch (1.3 cm) from the mark you have just made.

3. Use the Pushpin Method (page 19) and scissors to cut out the sections you have just marked on the paper-towel tube. Discard the top section.

4. Cut pieces of blue paper to cover each tube section. Each of the paper pieces should be 6 inches (15 cm) long and as high as the tube section it will cover.

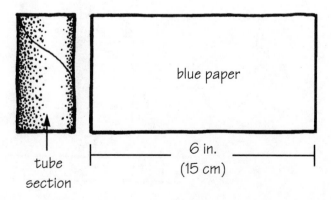

blue paper

tube section

6 in. (15 cm)

5. Coat the back of each piece of paper and the outside of each tube with stick glue. Press the paper onto the tubes, making sure to line up the edges of the paper with the edges of the tubes.

6. Squeeze a little white glue into the jar lid, and spread it around so you have a little puddle of glue.

7. Dip one end of each tube into the glue. Press the glued end of each tube against the top of one of the cans. Be sure to center the tubes on the can

tops. Two cans will not have tube bases.

8. Let the glue dry for about 15 minutes before going on to the next step.

9. Dip the other end of each tube into the glue and press each tube down onto the large piece of stiff cardboard or wood in the pattern shown in the diagram. Dip the bottoms of the two cans without tubes into the glue, and press them onto the cardboard, as shown.

10. Let the glue dry for about 15 minutes, and your hanukkiyah is done.

Note: This Hanukkiyah is just a decoration. Do not put candles on it.

✪ **Even Better:** Add orange or red construction paper "flames" to the tops of the cans.

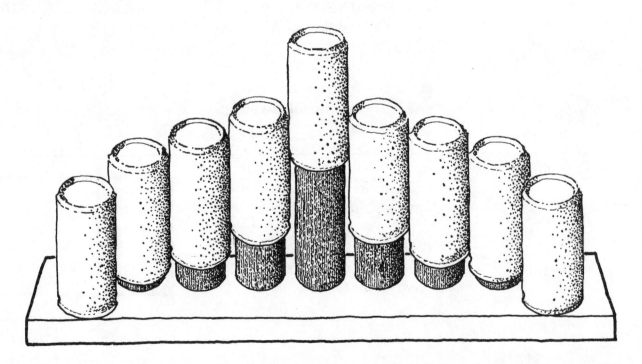

Christmas

*Christmas is celebrated on December 25th. It honors the birth of Jesus Christ,
and is one of the most important holidays of the Christian tradition.
The Christmas tree was adopted from a North European tradition
of decorating trees to celebrate the winter solstice
(the shortest day of the year).*

Paint-Blot Card

You can make this card by reusing one of the cards you received last year and making it over with a new paint-blot design.

You Need

❑ construction paper
❑ one recycled card (see the Card Method on page 12)
❑ poster paint in black, green, and white

Have on Hand

❑ stick glue

Tools

❑ an eraser
❑ a pencil
❑ a ruler
❑ scissors
❑ toothpicks

Instructions

1. Cut a piece of construction paper the same size as the front of your recycled card.

2. Fold the construction paper in half lengthwise.

3. Draw a light, tree-shaped guideline on half of the paper, using a ruler and pencil.

4. Using a toothpick, draw lines and dots with the green poster paint. Make all the lines and dots within the guideline.

5. After each line or dot is applied to one side, fold the paper together so that the paint is transferred to the other side. Open the paper at once.

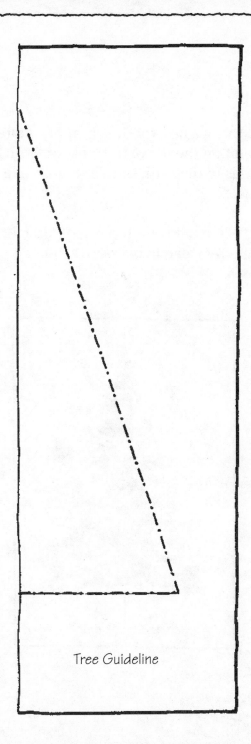

Tree Guideline

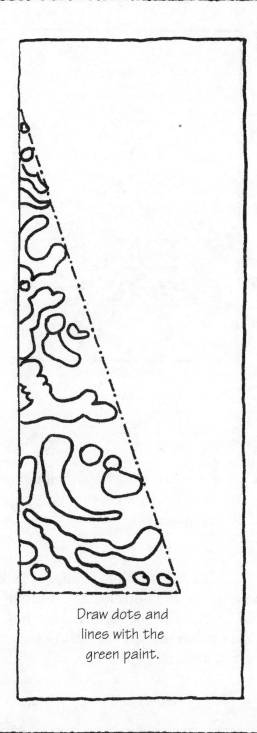

Draw dots and lines with the green paint.

green paint

8. Using a new toothpick, apply white paint on the top of the blots on both sides of the card, so that it looks like snow.

9. When the paint has dried (after 10 minutes), carefully erase the pencil lines.

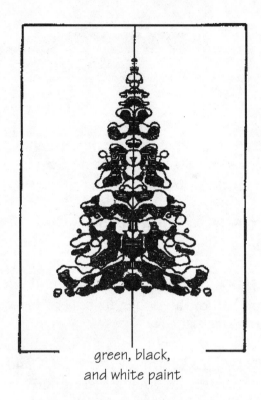

green, black, and white paint

6. Continue applying the green paint to fill out the tree area, but leave lots of empty space for the other two colors.

7. Using a new toothpick, apply black paint along the bottoms of the blots you made in steps **5** and **6**, including the blots on the left side of the paper. Do not fold the paper.

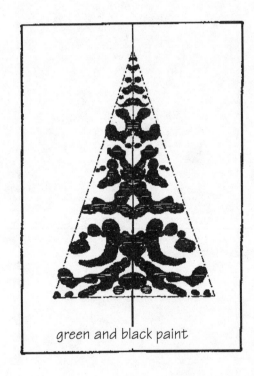

green and black paint

10. Glue the new design onto the front of the card.

✪ **Even Better:** Try other designs. Use a half-circle for a wreath or an ornament.

Photo Frame

Use a Styrofoam tray, a brown paper bag, and some gold foil from a chocolate bar to make a great-looking frame anyone would enjoy receiving for Christmas.

You Need

- ❏ a 3½ × 5-inch (8.8 × 12.5-cm) photo
- ❏ a clean, dry Styrofoam tray (such as from a food package), 6¼ × 8½ inches (15.6 × 21.3 cm) or larger
- ❏ a large brown paper bag
- ❏ gold foil with a paper back, such as from a candy bar
- ❏ scraps of black-colored paper from a magazine
- ❏ scrap cardboard

Have on Hand

- glue medium (see the Glue Medium Method on page 22)
- a bowl of warm water
- double-sided tape
- masking tape
- old newspaper
- an old towel or a clean rag

Tools

- a dinner knife
- a glue brush
- a hole punch
- a pushpin
- a ruler
- scissors

Instructions

1. Cover your work surface with newspaper to protect it.

2. Center the photo on the back of the Styrofoam tray. Mark the position of the photo by making pushpin holes at the corners, then remove the photo.

3. Make a second set of two pushpin holes ¼ inch (.6 cm) away from the first set of holes, as shown.

4. Use the ruler to draw lines connecting the second set of pushpin marks.

back of photo

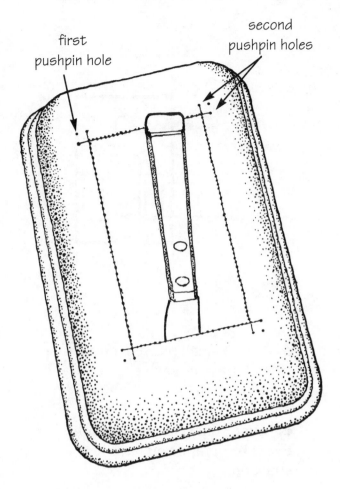

first
pushpin hole

second
pushpin holes

5. Use the Pushpin Method (see page 19) and the dinner knife to cut out the inside frame hole along the lines you have just marked. To make the corners neat, cut along each straight edge just to the corner. Discard the cutout piece.

6. To cover the frame with brown paper:

a. Soak the paper bag in a bowl of warm water for five minutes to soften it.

b. Remove the paper bag from the water and blot it with rags or a towel to remove any excess water.

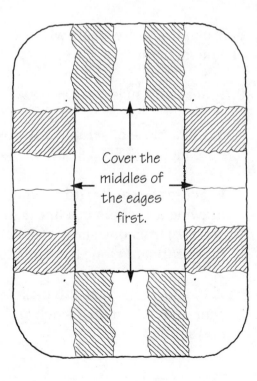

Cover the middles of the edges first.

c. Tear (do not cut) the damp paper into strips that are about 4 inches (10 cm) long and 2 inches (5 cm) wide.

d. Brush each strip of brown paper with glue medium. Also brush the frame under each strip.

e. Place strips onto the sides of the frame near the corners, as shown. Wrap each end of each strip around to the back of the frame. Brush an extra coat of medium over each strip.

f. Cover the rest of the frame, except the corners, with strips of brown paper. Be sure to overlap the edges of the strips.

g. Cover the corners by overlapping several small pieces, as shown. You may need to make small tears to wrap them around the corners.

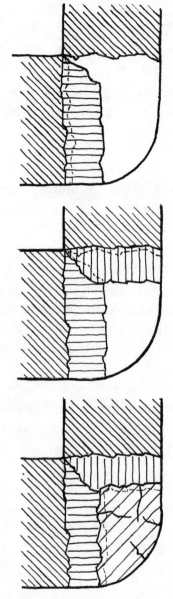

Cover the corners by overlapping several small pieces. You may need to make small tears to wrap them around the corners.

Note: As you cover the frame, make sure that strips already in place are stuck down firmly. If they aren't sticking, brush more glue medium onto them.

7. Tear the gold foil and black magazine paper into small bits. Glue them to the frame in a scatter pattern, as in the photo at the beginning of this project.

8. Brush the entire frame with a coat of glue medium.

9. To make a hanger:

   a. Cut a piece of scrap cardboard 1 × 1½ inches (2.5 × 3.8 cm).

   b. Score the cardboard by lightly drawing a pushpin in a line ½ inch (1.3 cm) from one short end. Fold the cardboard along the score line.

   c. Use the hole punch to make a centered hole in the ½-inch (1.3-cm) section.

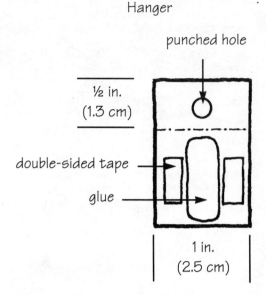

Hanger

punched hole

½ in. (1.3 cm)

double-sided tape

glue

1 in. (2.5 cm)

   d. Place a small piece of double-sided tape near each edge of the larger section.

   e. Brush some glue between the two tabs of tape you have just stuck on.

10. Glue the hanger to the top back of the frame, centered from side to side, with the hole end up. Let the glue dry for about 10 minutes.

11. Mount the photo into the back of the frame using masking tape.

Wrapping Bag

Lots of wrapping paper gets thrown away every Christmas. To keep from adding to the waste this year, make your wraps out of reused materials This bag is great looking and will hold a present of almost any size.

You Need

❑ two large, brown paper grocery bags

Have on Hand

❑ stick glue

Tools

❑ a hole punch
❑ a pencil
❑ scissors

Instructions

1. Cut the front panel off of one of the bags. Put aside the rest of the bag.

2. Fold the cutoff panel in half from side to side. Fold the folded bag in half again the same way.

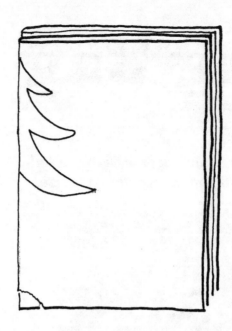

Line up the folded edge of the paper with the edge of the Tree Pattern.

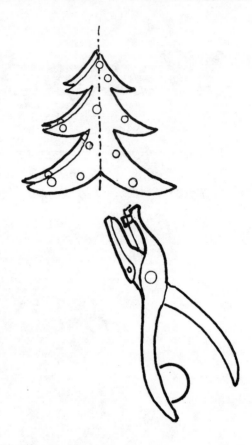

Tree
Pattern

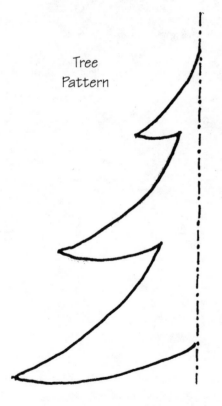

3. Use the Transfer Method (page 20) to transfer the Tree Pattern onto the cutoff bag panel. Be sure to line up the paper folds with the edges of the pattern, as shown.

4. Cut out the two paper trees. Start cutting at the fold, and be sure to cut through all four layers of paper.

5. Unfold the paper trees and use the hole punch to make several holes in each. The holes should be arranged to look like ornaments.

6. Glue the fold of one tree onto the front of the second bag, centered from side to side and a little closer to the top.

7. Glue the second tree overlapping the first tree, but a little further down the bag.

8. To make a handle:

   a. Cut one 3 × 12 inch (7.5 × 30-cm) strip from the leftover paper bag you put aside in step **1.**

   b. Fold the strip in half and glue the halves together.

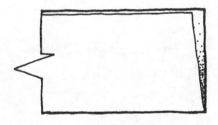

   c. Fold the strip in half again and glue the halves together.

d. Fold the ends of the strip down to make a handle, as shown.

9. Repeat step **8** to make a second handle.

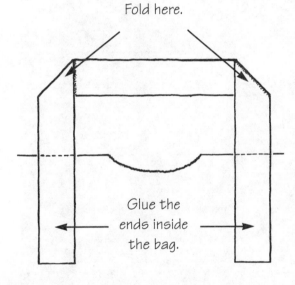

Fold here.

Glue the ends inside the bag.

10. Glue the handles to the insides of the sides of the bag, as shown.

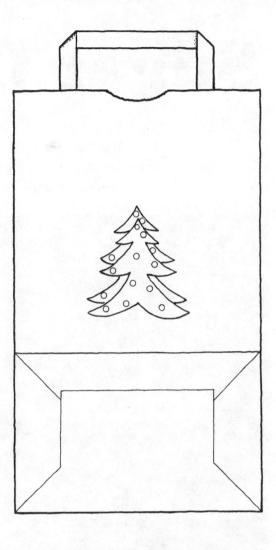

✪ **Even Better:** Instead of the trees, you can use other simple designs—like circles, wreaths, or candy canes—to decorate your Wrapping Bag.

Sugar Ornaments

You can make these beautiful ornaments from just sugar and food coloring, using the bottom of a plastic soda bottle as a mold.

You Need

- ❏ an empty 1-liter plastic soda bottle
- ❏ granulated sugar

Have on Hand

- ❏ a cookie sheet
- ❏ food coloring (any color)
- ❏ two mixing bowls
- ❏ scrap cardboard
- ❏ string
- ❏ ¾-inch (1.9-cm) masking tape
- ❏ white glue

Tools

- ❏ a fork
- ❏ a measuring cup
- ❏ measuring spoons
- ❏ a pushpin
- ❏ scissors
- ❏ a spoon

Instructions

1. Remove any labels from the soda bottle.

2. Wrap a piece of masking tape around the bottle, just below the ridge near the bottom, as shown.

3. Use the Pushpin Method (page 19) to cut around the bottle, along the bottom edge of the tape. The cut-off bottom will be your mold.

4. Measure 16 ounces (474 ml) of sugar and pour it into one mixing bowl.

5. Add 2 tablespoons (30 ml) of water to the bowl. Mix the sugar and water together with the fork until all the sugar is damp.

6. Spoon half the mixture into the second mixing bowl.

7. Add a drop of food coloring to the second bowl. Mix the food coloring into the damp sugar with the fork.

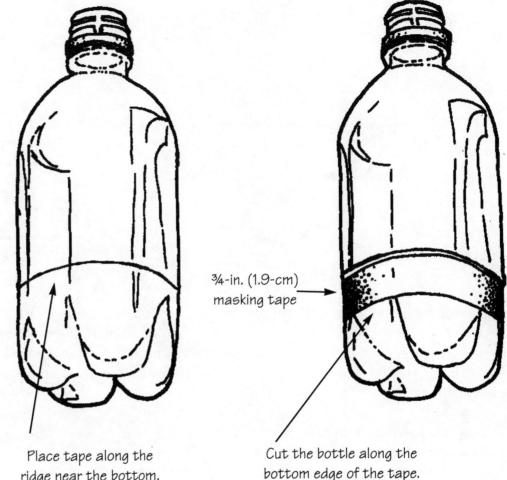

¾-in. (1.9-cm) masking tape

Place tape along the ridge near the bottom.

Cut the bottle along the bottom edge of the tape.

8. Spoon a layer of sugar from the first bowl into the mold. Use your fingers to press the sugar firmly into the bottom of the mold.

9. Add a layer of sugar from the second bowl on top of the layer from the first bowl. Use your fingers to press the second layer firmly into place.

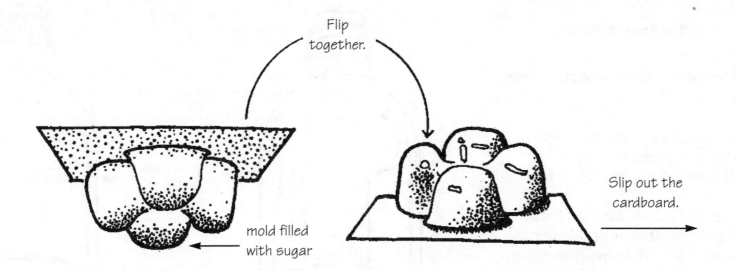

Flip together.

mold filled with sugar

Slip out the cardboard.

10. Keep adding damp sugar until the mold is filled.

11. Cover the top of the mold with a piece of cardboard.

12. Holding the cardboard in place, turn the mold over and place the mold and the cardboard onto the cookie sheet.

13. Carefully slip the cardboard out from under the mold.

14. Tap the top of the mold with your finger and carefully lift the mold off the sugar mixture. This is the first half of your ornament.

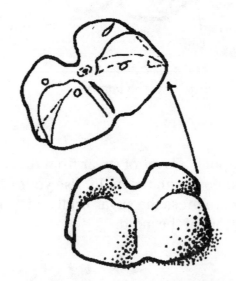

15. Repeat steps **4–14** to make the second half of the ornament.

16. Place the cookie sheet in a dry place where it will not be disturbed. Leave the ornaments to dry for two days. Do not try to lift the ornaments until they have dried completely.

17. Cut an 8-inch (2-cm) piece of string for each ornament. Tie the ends of the string together to make a loop.

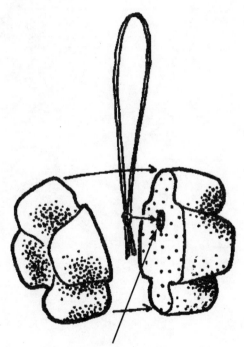

hole made with
a pushpin

18. Use the pushpin to scrape a small hole in the center of the back of one half of the ornament. The hole should be just as large as the knot in the string.

19. Use the pushpin to push the knot into the hole. Place a drop of glue on top of the knot to secure it in the hole.

20. Glue the two halves of the ornaments together back to back.

✪ **Even Better:** Find some other shapes to use as molds. Even the molds themselves can be hung on string and used as ornaments.

Kwanzaa

Kwanzaa, a holiday based on West African harvest celebrations, is celebrated from December 26th through January 1st. The word kwanzaa means "first fruits" in Swahili. The seven principles of Kwanzaa are umoja (unity); kujichagulia (self-determination); ujima (collective work and responsibility); ujamaa (cooperative economy); nia (purpose); kuuma (creativity); and imani (faith).

Ribbon Card

In the Kwanzaa tradition, the colors red, black, and green represent the blood in the veins of Africans, the color of Africans' skin, and the land of Africa. Remind your friends and family of the meaning of Kwanzaa with this recycled red, black, and green card.

You Need

- ❏ red, black, and green gift wrap ribbon, ¾ inch (2 cm) wide by 17 inches (43 cm)
- ❏ one recycled card (see the Card Method on page 12)
- ❏ an 8½ × 11-inch (22 × 27.5-cm) sheet of scrap paper

Have on Hand

- ❏ stick glue

Tools

- ❏ a pencil
- ❏ a ruler
- ❏ scissors

Instructions

1. Cut each 17-inch (43-cm) ribbon in half.

2. Glue the two green ribbons across opposite ends of the scrap paper, as shown. Make sure to apply glue along the entire length of the ribbons.

3. Glue the black ribbons next to, and just touching, the green ribbons.

4. Glue the red ribbons next to, and just touching, the black ribbons.

5. Cut the paper neatly along the outside edges of the red ribbons.

6. Put the ribbon sections face down on your work surface, with the red ribbons at the top.

7. Use the ruler and a pencil to draw the Ribbon Cutting Guide (page 121) onto the backs of the ribbon sections. Remember to make the lines slant in different directions on the two ribbon sections, as shown.

8. Use scissors to cut along the slanted lines you have just drawn. Be sure to keep the cutoff pieces in order.

9. Measure and mark the middle of the fold of the card. Make another mark in the middle of the opposite edge. Use the ruler and pencil to draw a faint line connecting the two marks you have just made.

10. Glue two 1½-inch (3.8-cm) ribbon strips on either side of the line you have just drawn. The ribbons on the

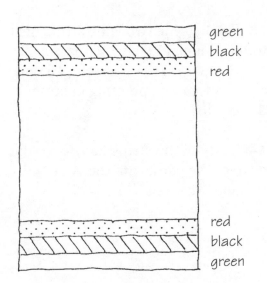

green
black
red

red
black
green

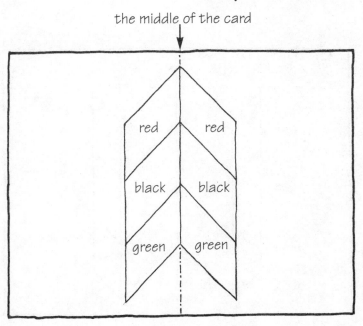

the middle of the card

red   red

black   black

green   green

two pieces should be slanting in different directions.

11. Glue two ¾-inch (1.9-cm) strips next to the 1½-inch (3.8-cm) strips. The ribbons should also be slanting in opposite directions.

12. Glue two more ¾-inch (1.9-cm) strips next to the ¾-inch (1.9-cm) strips you have just glued down. The ribbons on these new strips should be slanting in opposite directions.

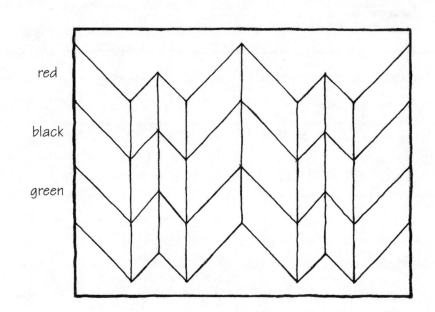

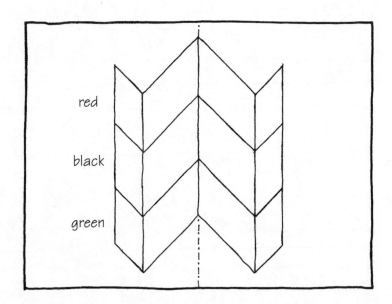

13. Finally, glue two wide strips next to the ¾-inch (1.9-cm) strips. Again, the ribbons on the 1½-inch (3.8-cm) strips should be pointing in opposite directions.

14. If any of the strips hang over the edge of the card, trim the edge straight with scissors.

Ribbon Cutting Guide

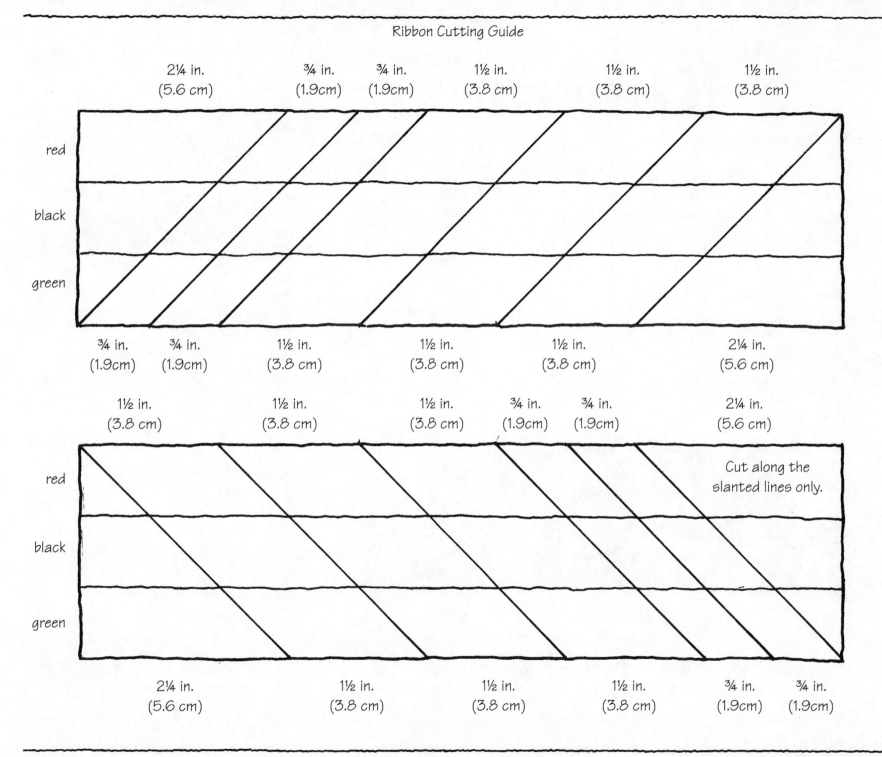

Top rectangle — top measurements (left to right):

2¼ in. (5.6 cm) · ¾ in. (1.9cm) · ¾ in. (1.9cm) · 1½ in. (3.8 cm) · 1½ in. (3.8 cm) · 1½ in. (3.8 cm)

Rows: red / black / green

Top rectangle — bottom measurements (left to right):

¾ in. (1.9cm) · ¾ in. (1.9cm) · 1½ in. (3.8 cm) · 1½ in. (3.8 cm) · 1½ in. (3.8 cm) · 2¼ in. (5.6 cm)

Bottom rectangle — top measurements (left to right):

1½ in. (3.8 cm) · 1½ in. (3.8 cm) · 1½ in. (3.8 cm) · ¾ in. (1.9cm) · ¾ in. (1.9cm) · 2¼ in. (5.6 cm)

Rows: red / black / green

Cut along the slanted lines only.

Bottom rectangle — bottom measurements (left to right):

2¼ in. (5.6 cm) · 1½ in. (3.8 cm) · 1½ in. (3.8 cm) · 1½ in. (3.8 cm) · ¾ in. (1.9cm) · ¾ in. (1.9cm)

Kinara

Kinara *is the Swahili word for "cornstalk."*
The Kwanzaa kinara holds seven candles, which represent
the nguzo saba, *the seven principles of Kwanzaa.*

You Need

- ❏ three identical clear glass jars with lids, about 4½ inches (11.3 cm) tall (such as jam jars)
- ❏ two identical clear glass jars with lids, about 5¼ inches (13 cm) tall (such as jam jars)
- ❏ two clear glass jars with lids, about 3½ inches (7.5 cm) tall (such as salsa jars)
- ❏ recycled tissue paper, in black, red, and green, cut into 4-inch (10-cm) squares
- ❏ ¾-inch (1.9-cm) gift-wrap ribbon, in black, red, and green

Have on Hand

- ❏ double-sided tape

Tools

- ❏ scissors

Instructions

1. Wash the jars thoroughly inside and out. Remove any labels from the jars. (You may need to soak the jars in water overnight to remove the labels.)

Loosely crumple pieces of tissue paper and push them into the jars.

2. Loosely crumple pieces of tissue paper and push them into the jars. Put the lids back on the jars. You don't need a lot of tissue—look at the photo at the beginning of this project as a guide.

> **a.** Fill one of each size jar with four red tissues.
>
> **b.** Fill one of each size jar with four green tissues.
>
> **c.** Fill the remaining jar with four black tissues.

3. Place a small piece of double-sided tape on the sides of each of the jar lids.

4. Wrap a ribbon around each of the jar lids—red on the jars filled with red tissue, green for the green jars, and black for the black jar.

> **a.** Stick one end of the ribbon to the tape you put on the jar in step **3**.
>
> **b.** Wrap the ribbon around the jar once.

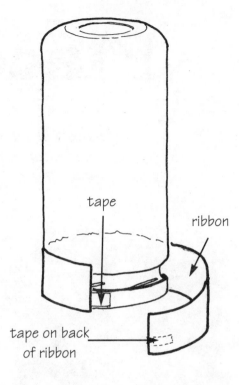

tape

ribbon

tape on back of ribbon

> **c.** Cut the ribbon a little beyond the point where it overlaps.
>
> **d.** Stick the loose end of the ribbon down with a piece of double-sided tape.

5. Arrange the jars as shown in the photo at the beginning of this project—with the black jar in the middle, the three green jars on one side, and the three red jars on the other side.

6. Your kinara is ready.

Place Mats

*This place mat will remind you of the meaning of
the Kwanzaa colors at every meal.*

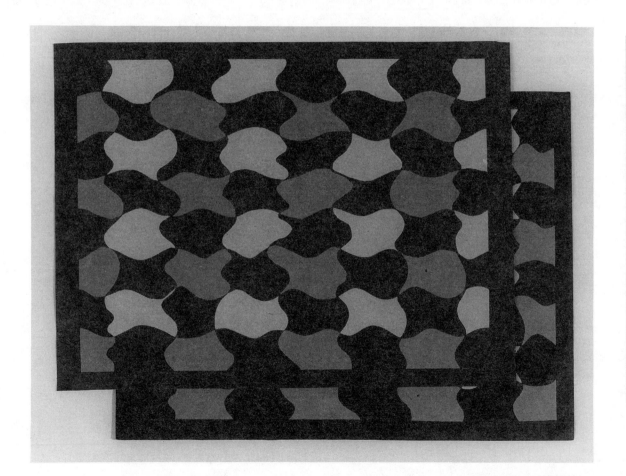

You Need

❑ four sheets of 9 × 12-inch
(22.5 × 30-cm) construction
paper: two black, one red,
and one green

Have on Hand

❑ stick glue

Tools

❑ a pencil
❑ a ruler
❑ scissors

Instructions

1. On one piece of black construction paper, measure and mark points ½ inch (1.3 cm) along the edges from each corner. Draw light pencil lines connecting the marks you have made to form a rectangular border.

2. Along one short end of the paper, measure and mark every 1 inch (2.5 cm) inside the lines you have just drawn.

3. Repeat on the other short end of the paper, starting from the same edge.

4. Use the ruler and pencil to draw lines connecting the marks you have just made.

5. Using the straight lines as a guide, draw wavy lines over the straight lines.

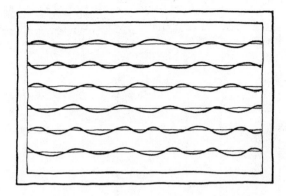

Cut along the wavy lines.

6. Cut along the wavy lines you have just marked. Do not cut into the borders.

7. Cut along the long-side border lines you drew in step **1**. Cut a little past the end border.

8. Cut the red and green pieces of construction paper down to 11 inches (27.5 cm) long. Recycle the cutoff scraps.

9. Tape the red construction paper on top of the green construction paper. It is very important that the edges of the two pieces line up exactly.

black paper

½ in. (1.3 cm)

1 in. (2.5 cm)

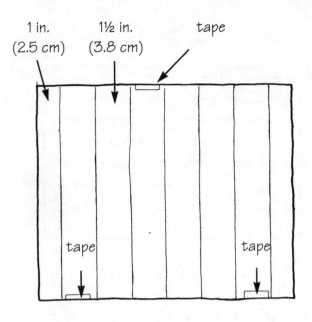

1 in.
(2.5 cm)

1½ in.
(3.8 cm)

tape

tape

tape

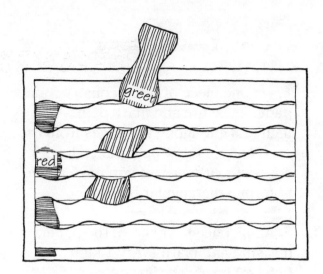

green

red

10. Measure and mark points 1 inch (2.5 cm) along the sides from each short end of the taped-together paper. Draw lines connecting these marks.

11. On both long sides of the paper, make a mark every 1½ inches (3.8 cm) between the lines you have just drawn. Draw lines connecting these marks.

12. Draw wavy lines centered on the straight lines you have just drawn.

13. Cut along the wavy lines with scissors. Make sure you cut through both pieces of paper at the same time. As you cut off each piece, lay it down on your work surface. Lay the pieces down in the same order that you cut them out, so that they will fit together later.

14. Separate the pairs of red and green pieces, keeping them in order.

15. Weave red and green pieces through the wavy lines in the black piece, alternating colors. Start and

Cut along the wavy lines. Make sure to cut through both pieces of paper.

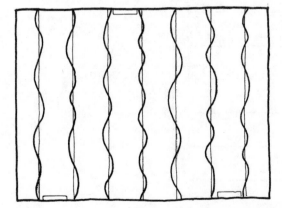

finish with the 1-inch (2.5-cm) -wide pieces. Make sure all your weaves start and end on the same side of the black paper.

16. Glue the ends of the red and green strips to the black paper using stick glue.

17. Turn the mat over, and it's ready.

18. Make a second mat by repeating steps **1–7** with the second piece of black paper and steps **15** and **16** with the leftover red and green strips.

Staying Earth-Friendly

In this book there are facts and tips about trash, recycling, and how you can help save the Earth.

If you want more information about how you can help, you can write to the groups listed here. These organizations can give you ideas and information about reducing, reusing, and recycling.

Don't forget your local resources. Parents, teachers, neighbors, and friends probably have lots of information about how your community recycles.

Organizations

Coalition for a Recyclable Waste Stream
1525 New Hampshire Ave., NW
Washington, DC 20036
(301) 891-1100

The Environmental Action Coalition
625 Broadway, Second Floor
New York, NY 10012
(212) 677-1601

Environmental Defense Fund
475 Park Ave. South
New York, NY 10016
(800) CALL-EDF

Inform
381 Park Ave. South
New York, NY 10016
(212) 689-4040

Keep America Beautiful
Mill River Plaza
9 West Broad St.
Stamford, CT 06902
(203) 323-8987

National Recycling Coalition
1101 30th St., NW
Washington, DC 20007
(202) 625-6406

Natural Resource Defense Council
40 West 20th St.
New York, NY 10011
(212) 727-2700

Other Books

If you've enjoyed reading *Earth-Friendly Holidays*, you might also enjoy these books:

About Garbage and Stuff
Ann A. Shanks, Viking Press,
New York, 1973.

Cartons, Cans, and Orange Peels:
Where Does Your Garbage Go?
Joanna Foster, Clarion Books,
New York, 1991.

Earth Book for Kids: Activities
to Help Heal the Environment
Linda Schwartz, The Learning Works,
Santa Barbara, Calif., 1990.

The Kid's Guide to Social Action
Barbara A. Lewis, Free Spirit
Publishing, Minneapolis, 1991.

The Lorax
Dr. Seuss, Random House, New York,
1988.

Taking Out the Trash:
A No-Nonsense Guide to Recycling
Jennifer Carfess, Island Press,
Washington, D.C., 1992.